Prepared in cooperation with the
New Hampshire Department of Environmental Services

Methods for Estimating Withdrawal and Return Flow by Census Block for 2005 and 2020 for New Hampshire

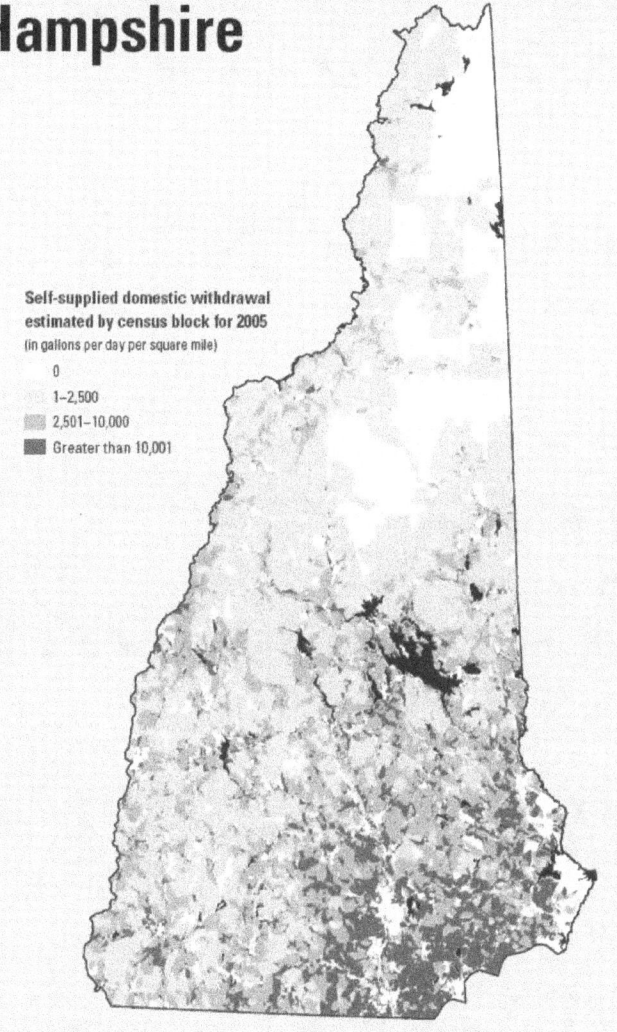

Self-supplied domestic withdrawal
estimated by census block for 2005
(in gallons per day per square mile)

    0
    1–2,500
    2,501–10,000
    Greater than 10,001

Open-File Report 2009–1168

U.S. Department of the Interior
U.S. Geological Survey

Cover. Map shows the intensity of self-supplied domestic withdrawal estimated by census block for 2005 in New Hampshire.

Methods for Estimating Withdrawal and Return Flow by Census Block for 2005 and 2020 for New Hampshire

By Laura Hayes and Marilee A. Horn

Prepared in cooperation with the
New Hampshire Department of Environmental Services

Open-File Report 2009–1168

U.S. Department of the Interior
U.S. Geological Survey

U.S. Department of the Interior
KEN SALAZAR, Secretary

U.S. Geological Survey
Marcia K. McNutt, Director

U.S. Geological Survey, Reston, Virginia: 2009

For more information on the USGS—the Federal source for science about the Earth, its natural and living resources, natural hazards, and the environment, visit http://www.usgs.gov or call 1-888-ASK-USGS

For an overview of USGS information products, including maps, imagery, and publications, visit http://www.usgs.gov/pubprod

To order this and other USGS information products, visit http://store.usgs.gov

Suggested citation:
Hayes, Laura, and Horn, M.A., 2009, Methods for estimating withdrawal and return flow by census block for 2005 and 2020 for New Hampshire: U.S. Geological Survey Open-File Report 2009–1168, 32 p., available at http://pubs.usgs.gov/of/2009/1168.

Acknowledgments

This project has been carried out with support from Sarah Pillsbury and Brandon Kernen of the New Hampshire Department of Environmental Services (NHDES). The authors would like to thank Johnna McKenna of NHDES for providing the Water Distribution and Sewer Collection Areas geographic information systems data, Linda Thompson of New Hampshire Drinking Water and Groundwater Bureau for providing a copy of the Drinking Water database, Frederick Chormann of the New Hampshire Geological Survey/NHDES for providing a copy of the state water-use registration database (WATUSE), and Daniel Dudley of NHDES for providing a copy of the National Pollutant Discharge Elimination System (NPDES) wastewater facility database.

We would also like to thank Leslie DeSimone and Mark Nardi of the U.S. Geological Survey (USGS) for their critical reviews of the report. Appreciation also is extended to the following USGS employees: Kim Otto and Ruth Larkins for editorial reviews, Susan Bergin and Christine Mendelsohn for illustrations, and Ann Marie Squillacci for manuscript preparation and layout.

Contents

Figures

Tables

Conversion Factors, Datum, and Acronyms

Multiply	By	To obtain
Length		
foot (ft)	0.3048	meter (m)
Area		
acre	4,047	square meter (m^2)
acre	0.004047	square kilometer (km^2)
square mile (mi^2)	2.590	square kilometer (km^2)
Volume		
gallon (gal)	3.785	liter (L)
gallon (gal)	0.003785	cubic meter (m^3)
Flow rate		
gallon per day (gal/d)	0.003785	cubic meter per day (m^3/d)
million gallons per day (Mgal/d)	0.04381	cubic meter per second (m^3/s)

Horizontal coordinate information is referenced to the North American Datum of 1983 (NAD 83).

ACRONYMS USED IN REPORT

CFCC	Census Feature Class Code
CWS	community water system
CWWS	community wastewater system
FIPS	Federal Information Processing Standards
GIS	geographic information system
MCD	minor civil division
NCWS	non-community water system
NHDES	New Hampshire Department of Environmental Services
NHDWGB	New Hampshire Drinking Water and Groundwater Bureau
NHGS	New Hampshire Geological Survey
NHOEP	New Hampshire Office of Energy and Planning
NHWEB	New Hampshire Wastewater Engineering Bureau
NPDES	National Pollutant Discharge Elimination System
PWSID	Public Water System identification number
SDWA	Safe Drinking Water Act
SDWP	Safe Drinking Water Program
SIC	Standard Industrial Classification
STFID	census block (Summary Tape File) identification number
TIGER	Topologically Integrated Geographic Encoding and Referencing
USEPA	United States Environmental Protection Agency
USGS	United States Geological Survey
WATUSE	water-use database maintained by the New Hampshire Geological Survey
WWTF	wastewater-treatment facility

Methods for Estimating Withdrawal and Return Flow by Census Block for 2005 and 2020 for New Hampshire

By Laura Hayes and Marilee A. Horn

Abstract

The U.S. Geological Survey, in cooperation with the New Hampshire Department of Environmental Services, estimated the amount of water demand, consumptive use, withdrawal, and return flow for each U.S. Census block in New Hampshire for the years 2005 (current) and 2020. Estimates of domestic, commercial, industrial, irrigation, and other nondomestic water use were derived through the use and innovative integration of several State and Federal databases, and by use of previously developed techniques.

The New Hampshire Water Demand database was created as part of this study to store and integrate State of New Hampshire data central to the project. Within the New Hampshire Water Demand database, a lookup table was created to link the State databases and identify water users common to more than one database. The lookup table also allowed identification of withdrawal and return-flow locations of registered and unregistered commercial, industrial, agricultural, and other nondomestic users. Geographic information system data from the State were used in combination with U.S. Census Bureau spatial data to locate and quantify withdrawals and return flow for domestic users in each census block.

Analyzing and processing the most recently available data resulted in census-block estimations of 2005 water use. Applying population projections developed by the State to the data sets enabled projection of water use for the year 2020. The results for each census block are stored in the New Hampshire Water Demand database and may be aggregated to larger political areas or watersheds to assess relative hydrologic stress on the basis of current and potential water availability.

Introduction

The New Hampshire Department of Environmental Services (NHDES) is developing a systematic, statewide assessment to quantify indicators of hydrologic stress at the level of individual stream segments and the areas that drain directly to these features. These local-scale data can be aggregated to larger areas and higher levels of organization within a hierarchy of watersheds to support regional assessments as needed.

The approach used by NHDES defines hydrologic stress as the ratio of cumulative net water withdrawal to estimated natural streamflow for each stream reach. Water withdrawal and return flow in New Hampshire must be quantified for assessing hydrologic stress. Registered water use (water withdrawn, used, or returned by facilities that use at least 20,000 gal of water per day) is known because monthly pumpage is reported to the New Hampshire Geological Survey (NHGS) on a quarterly basis. The amount of water withdrawn and returned by those using less than 20,000 gal of water per day (unregistered users) is unknown and has not been estimated statewide. The U.S. Geological Survey (USGS) developed procedures for estimating unregistered water use as part of a detailed water-use analysis for the Seacoast region of New Hampshire (Horn and others, 2008). Estimates of all withdrawals and return flow can be made by combining the reported withdrawal and return-flow data for registered users with estimates of water use for unregistered users. NHDES also would like to assess potential water demand for 2020 and relate this demand to natural streamflows. To aid the water-resource planning efforts of NHDES, the USGS generated estimates of (1) current (2005) unregistered water withdrawal and return flow and (2) future (2020) total water withdrawal and return flow by census block throughout the State.

Purpose and Scope

This report details the methods used to estimate water withdrawal and return flow in 2005 and project water withdrawal and return flow for 2020 throughout the State of New Hampshire by U.S. Census block. The report also describes the New Hampshire Water Demand database, which was created during this study and contains versions of State databases that are linked through a new lookup table. Water-use activities evaluated include water withdrawal, delivery, demand, consumptive use, release, return flow, and transfer (for an explanation of these water-use terms, see section entitled "Water-Use Concepts" and (or) the glossary).

Water-Use Concepts

In this report, water use generally refers to specific activities that involve the use of water by humans. Water-use activities begin when water is diverted or withdrawn from surface-water or groundwater sources and conveyed to a place of use (fig. 1). A withdrawal is made by an individual user or by a community water system (CWS) that may treat the water and convey (deliver) it to users through a distribution system (Horn, 2002). A CWS is defined as a public water system that delivers water for human consumption through pipes and other constructed conveyances and regularly serves at least 25 year-round residents or has at least 15 service connections used by year-round residents (U.S. Environmental Protection Agency, 1998). CWSs might serve towns, cities, military bases, apartment complexes, or mobile home parks. Users who obtain their water directly from a groundwater or surface-water source, and not from a CWS, are self-supplied. In this report, CWSs are divided into two groups: domestic CWSs that serve only domestic users in mobile-home parks, condominiums, and other residential developments, and multi-use CWSs that serve a mix of domestic, commercial, industrial, and irrigation users (Horn and others, 2008).

A non-community water system (NCWS) is a different type of public water system that serves people either temporarily in residence (transient), as at a motel or restaurant, or regularly using the drinking-water supply without actually living at the site (nontransient), as at a business. For the purposes of estimating water demand in this report, the NCWSs are treated not as public water systems but as water users, because NCWSs use water at their location (unlike CWSs, which deliver water to other entities to use). Note that they are considered public water systems when discussing them in the context of the Safe Drinking Water Program (SDWP) and the Drinking Water database that supports the SDWP.

Water demand refers to water that is needed or used for a specific purpose by a single user or aggregate of users within a geographic area. Examples include domestic activities in a household (such as drinking or bathing), irrigation, or industrial processing. In this study, nine categories of water demand were estimated—domestic, commercial, industrial, golf-course irrigation, agricultural irrigation, hydroelectric, thermoelectric, mining, and aquaculture. Nondomestic water demand in this report refers to the eight categories of use other than domestic demand.

Consumptive use refers to water that evaporates during use or is incorporated into a product and, therefore, is removed from the immediate environment. Unaccounted-for water use refers to water in a distribution system that leaks back into the hydrologic system, is used in firefighting, or is used for infrastructure maintenance (street cleaning, filter backwash at the treatment plant, or hydrant and system flushing) (Horn, 2002).

Wastewater can be returned by a user directly to the groundwater system through on-lot (septic) sewage disposal systems. It also can be returned to groundwater or surface water from the treatment facility of a community wastewater system (CWWS) after the users have released their wastewater to sewers and the wastewater has been conveyed to the treatment facility. Finally, wastewater can be returned from industrial and other nondomestic on-site wastewater-treatment systems to surface water or groundwater. All of these wastewater pathways are collectively called return flow (Horn and others, 2008).

Water also can be transferred from one area into another—water leaving an area (political or drainage basin) is termed an export, and water entering an area is termed an import. Water moved from one watershed to another is called an interbasin transfer.

A state or any region may be divided into various geographic units for the purpose of grouping the users and estimating the amount of water use in each unit. In this report, three primary geographic divisions are considered: census blocks, minor civil divisions (MCDs), and watersheds. A census block is a geographic subdivision of a census block group and is the smallest geographic area for which the U.S. Census Bureau collects and tabulates population and housing counts (U.S. Census Bureau, 2007). The census block provides the most flexible basis for compiling water-use data, because it can be aggregated to many different watershed or political hierarchies and can be updated with information from more accurate and detailed studies as they become available. New Hampshire is made up of 34,728 census blocks; the average census block area is 0.27 mi^2 or about 170 acres. In urban areas, a census block can be visualized as a rectangular plot of land surrounded by streets on four sides, about 4 acres in area. In rural areas where there is no street grid, census blocks are bounded by streets, streams, political boundaries, or even former railroad rights-of-way or power lines and can range in area up to several thousand acres. A MCD is a type of governmental unit that is the primary legal or administrative subdivision of a county (U.S. Census Bureau, 2007). In New Hampshire, MCDs are generally equivalent to towns except that some MCDs are unincorporated. A watershed is a geographic area that drains water to one outlet point. Watersheds can be subdivided into smaller drainage areas.

Methods for Estimating Water Use

Estimates of water use rely on understanding what factors influence water demand and its associated consumptive use, because changes in demand and consumptive use affect withdrawal and return flow. At the simplest level, the methods for estimating water demand can be grouped into three basic steps: (1) identifying the water users, (2) determining areas where withdrawal and return flow occur, and (3) estimating amounts of water demand and consumptive use to derive withdrawal and return flow.

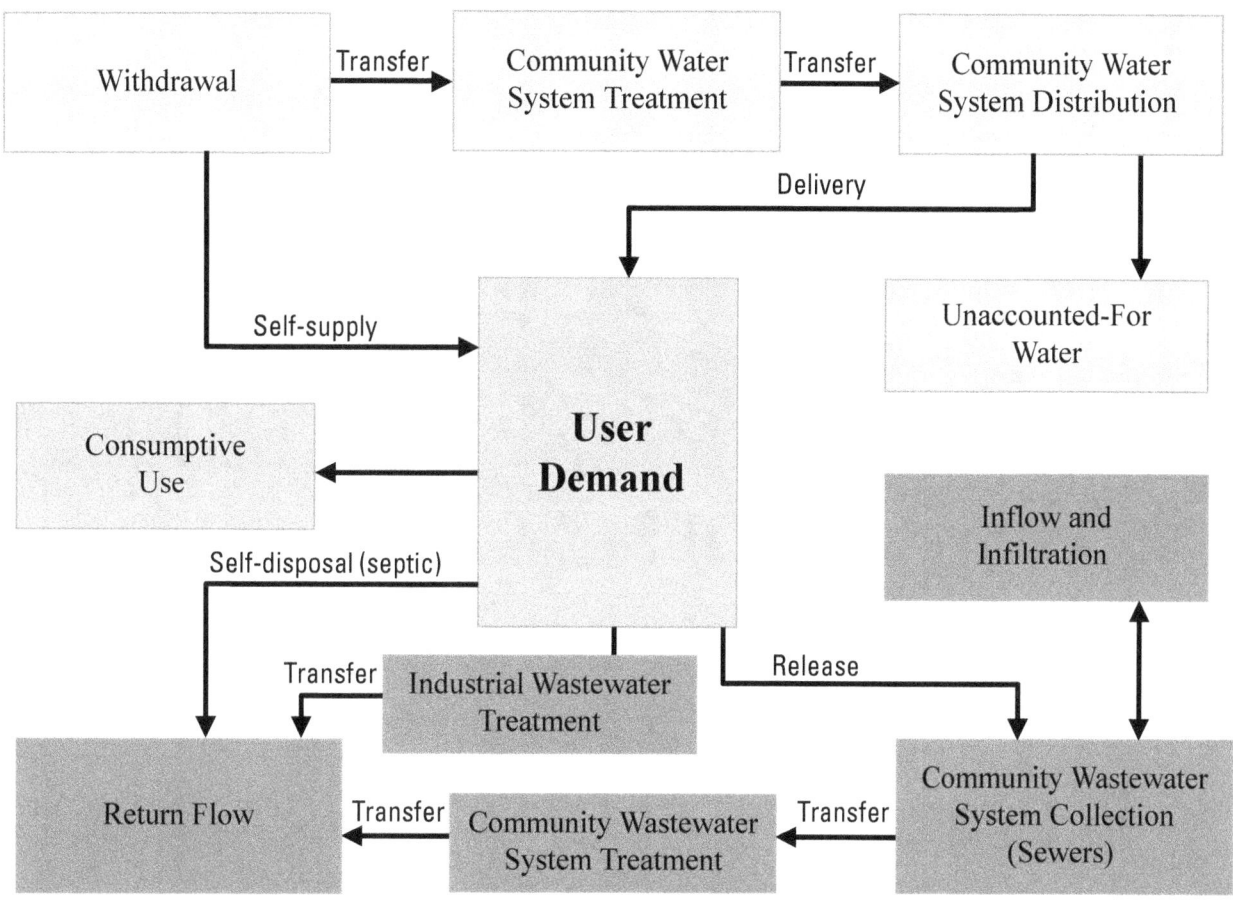

Figure 1. Relations among water-use activities. [Conveyance is represented in the flowchart by arrows. (Modified from Horn, 2002)].

Identifying Water Users

Water users in New Hampshire were identified through compilation and analysis of water-use and related data from State and Federal databases. Three State programs in New Hampshire maintain databases used in identifying who withdraws and (or) returns water. These programs and databases include (1) NHGS's water-use registration and reporting program and the State water-use database (WATUSE); (2) the New Hampshire Drinking Water and Groundwater Bureau (NHDWGB) and the Drinking Water database; and (3) the New Hampshire Wastewater Engineering Bureau (NHWEB) and the National Pollutant Discharge Elimination System (NPDES) databases. Population data and geographic-boundary files were obtained from the U.S. Census Bureau. Population estimates for 2005 and population projections for 2020 for MCDs were obtained from the New Hampshire Office of Energy and Planning (NHOEP) (fig. 2). All of the data collected for the study are stored and linked in the New Hampshire Water Demand database.

WATUSE Database

In 1987, New Hampshire State law established a water-use registration and reporting program to gather data on the largest water users in the State (New Hampshire Geological Survey, 2007). This information is used by the State to assess water demand on the State's aquifers, lakes, reservoirs, rivers, and streams. All facilities that use more than 20,000 gal/d averaged over any 7-day period or 600,000 gal in any 30-day period are required to register and report their monthly water withdrawal, delivery, release to sewers, and return flow by each source and destination. The program is now administered by the NHGS. Data on the registrants and their reported water use are stored in the State WATUSE database. A copy of the WATUSE database with reported water use for 2005 was obtained from NHDES (Frederick Chormann, written commun., 2006) in October 2006.

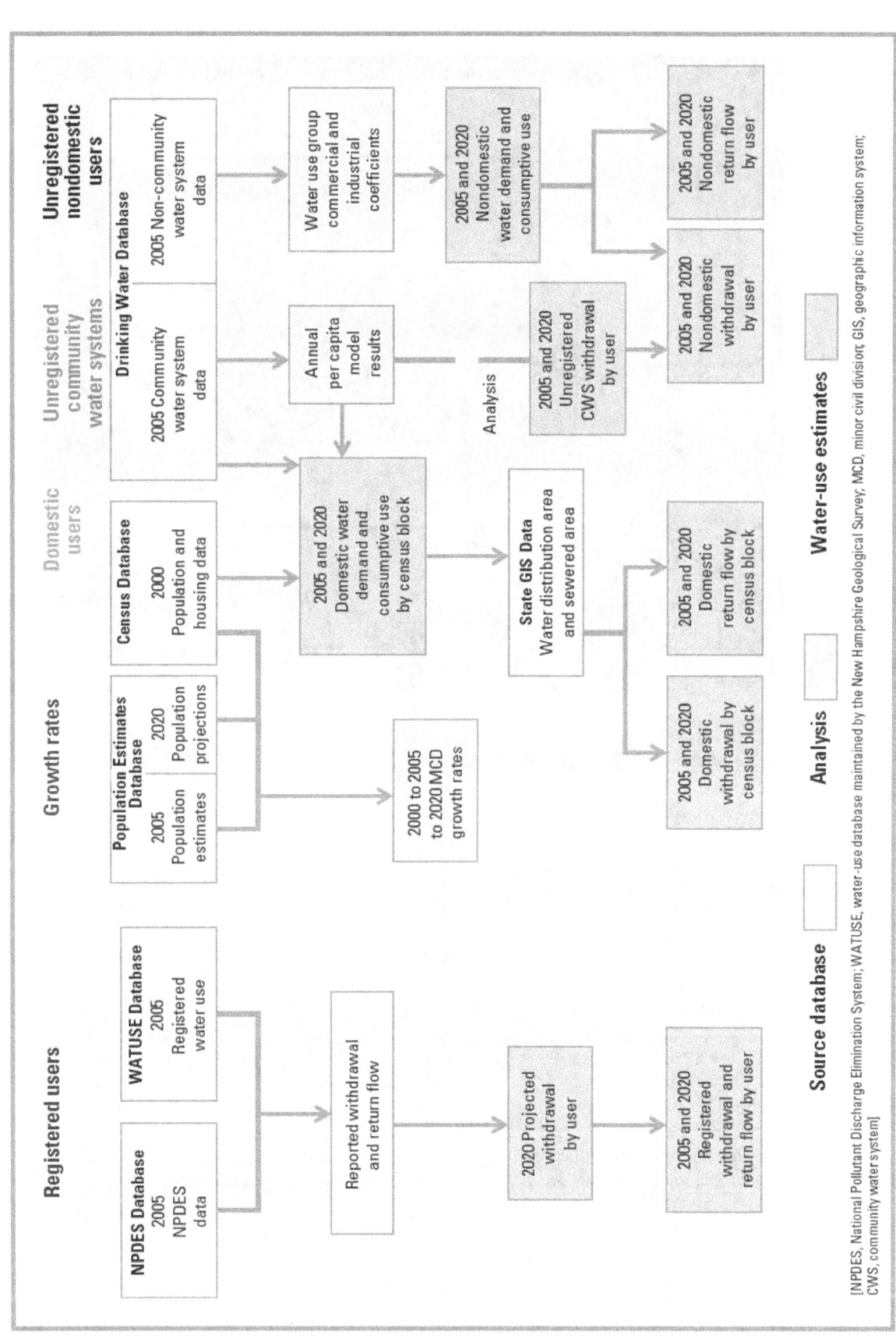

Figure 2. Approach and data sets used in estimating withdrawal and return flow by census block in New Hampshire.

[NPDES, National Pollutant Discharge Elimination System; WATUSE, water-use database maintained by the New Hampshire Geological Survey; MCD, minor civil division; GIS, geographic information system; CWS, community water system]

Drinking Water Database

The NHDWGB has the responsibility to administer the Federal Safe Drinking Water Act (SDWA) and other statutes related to public drinking-water supplies. In order to support this program responsibility, the NHDWGB maintains a Drinking Water database of information on public water systems. The database contains information on population served, contact addresses, locations of sources, and details about status and types of systems and sources. A copy of the Drinking Water database was obtained from NHDWGB (Linda Thompson, written commun., 2007) in March 2007.

NPDES Databases

The NHWEB has the responsibility of working with the U.S. Environmental Protection Agency (USEPA) in support of the NPDES permit program under the Clean Water Act. The responsibility of the NHWEB is to ensure that the operation and maintenance of wastewater-treatment facilities (WWTFs) are in accordance with the Federal NPDES discharge permits for each facility by providing compliance inspections, technical assistance, operator training, and operator certification (New Hampshire Department of Environmental Services, 2006). Furthermore, the NHWEB certifies discharge permits under the Federal NPDES permit program to ensure that the wastewater discharges do not violate applicable State rules and regulations. In order to support this program responsibility, the NHWEB maintains the NPDES databases. These databases include information on wastewater facilities, such as contact addresses, locations of discharge pipes, and details about status and types of systems. Copies of the NPDES databases were obtained from NHDES (Daniel Dudley, written commun., 2007) in December 2007.

Census Database

Data were obtained from the U.S. Census Bureau in both tabular and spatial formats (U.S. Census Bureau, 2001, 2006). The population and housing-unit data from tabular census files, collectively known as Summary File 1, were joined to the spatial representation of census blocks. The census data sets are the most accurate, best documented demographic and housing data available and are associated with geographic regions at multiple scales.

Population Estimates Database

The NHOEP develops and maintains databases of population estimates for years between the official decennial counts by the U.S. Census Bureau and of projections for future years (New Hampshire Office of Energy and Planning, 2007a, 2007b). Population estimates for the year 2005 and population projections for the year 2020 were obtained from these databases for each MCD.

The New Hampshire Water Demand Database

The New Hampshire (NH) Water Demand database was developed in Microsoft Access as a tool to integrate and analyze water-use data. An overview of the structure of the NH Water Demand database, including the relations among individual tables, is shown in figure 3. The database includes tables from the three State water-use databases, the Census database, and the Population Estimates database, plus links to the State geographic information system (GIS) data on CWS distribution and CWWS collection systems (yellow boxes in fig. 3). Tables that were created during the processing and manipulating of the source data, including data from GIS analyses, are also part of the NH Water Demand database and are represented by blue boxes in figure 3. These tables are named and described in table 1. Queries were developed to create the final results (green boxes in fig. 3).

The three State databases (WATUSE, Drinking Water, and NPDES) were linked together to ensure that withdrawal and return flow by individual users were not double counted (and that if a reported value was available, an estimated value was not required). Facilities that were common to any two of the three databases were identified, and a lookup table called the State Databases Index (fig. 4) was established. The number of facilities in New Hampshire common to multiple databases is shown in figure 5. Table 2 shows an example of information for a facility in all three databases. In addition to identifying unique facilities, linking the State databases also ensured that each point of withdrawal and return is unique in the NH Water Demand database.

In table 2, the unique identification numbers for facilities and source/destination points are provided as examples. In WATUSE, each registered facility has a unique 5-digit number (WU_ID), beginning with a "2." Each source in WATUSE has a unique identification number (Source_ID) containing the WU_ID, followed by a dash, the letter "S," and a 2-digit number, such as "01." Each destination has a unique identification number (Destination_ID) containing the WU_ID, followed by a dash, the letter "D," and a 2-digit number, such as "01." In the Drinking Water database, each public water system has a unique 7-digit identification number (PWSID). Each source in the Drinking Water database has a unique identification number (Source_Entity_ID) containing the PWSID, followed by a dash and a 7-digit number, such as "0000002." In the NPDES database, each facility has a unique identification number (NPDES_ID), which has nine alpha-numeric characters beginning with "NH." Each destination (discharge point) in the NPDES database has a unique identification number (Discharge_Entity_ID) in one of a variety of formats.

In addition to identifying common facilities, it was necessary to create a link in the State Databases Index table between points of withdrawal in each database and points of return flow in each database to ensure that reported data were properly included in the final water-use estimates. Water sources and discharge points common to more than one State

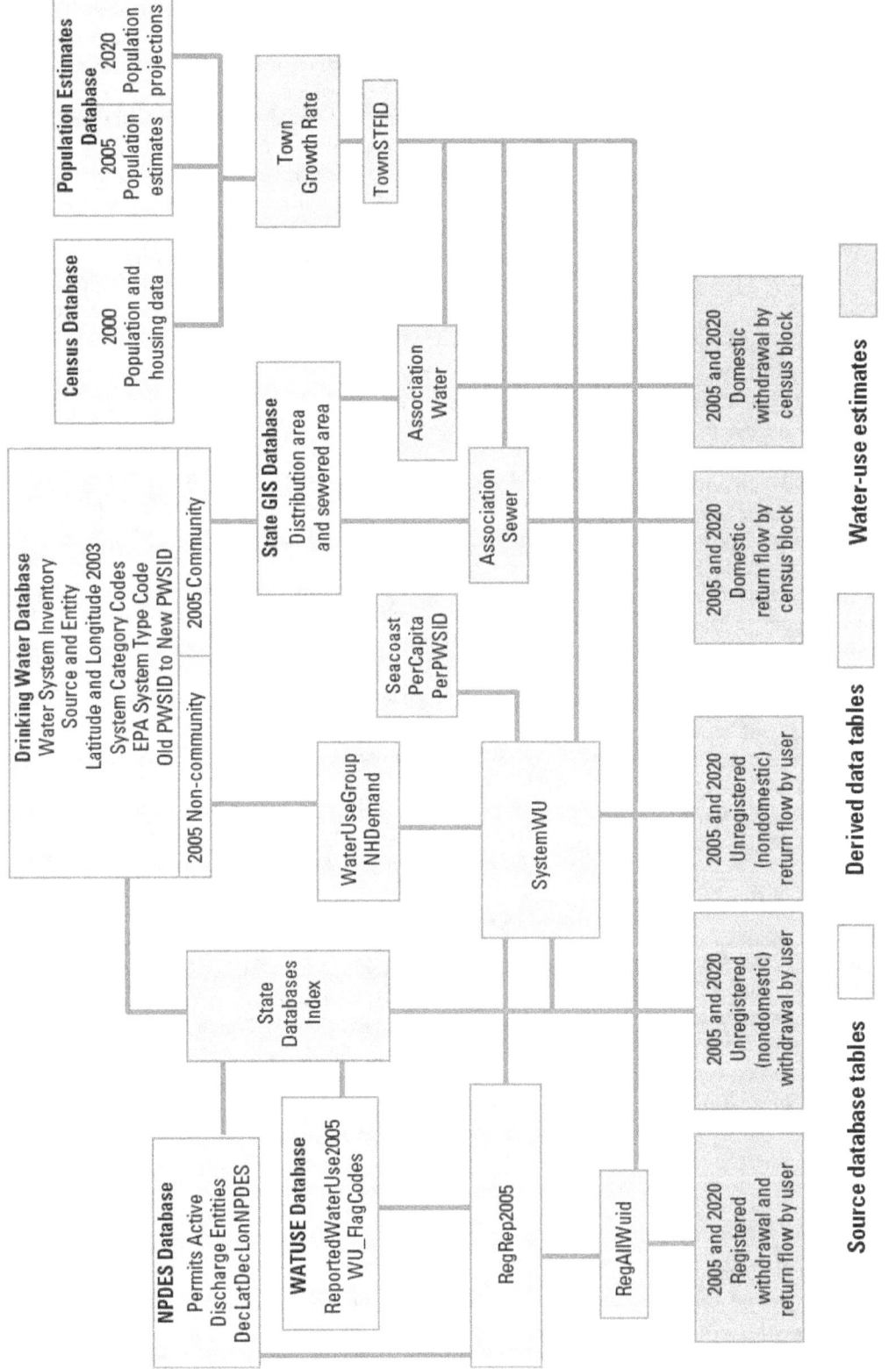

Figure 3. Table structure of the New Hampshire Water Demand database.

[USEPA, United States Environmental Protection Agency; PWSID, Public Water System identification number; GIS, geographic information system; STFID, census block identification number; WU, water use; [Derived data tables are described in table 1.]]

Table 1. Derived data tables in the New Hampshire Water Demand database.

[WATUSE, water-use database maintained by the New Hampshire Geological Survey; NPDES, National Pollutant Discharge Elimination System; STFID, census block identification number; SIC, Standard Industrial Classification; PWSID, Public Water System identification number; GIS, geographic information system; CWS, community water system; CWWS, community wastewater system; WU_ID, Unique number assigned to the water user in the WATUSE database; NPDES_ID, National Pollutant Discharge Elimination System identification number]

Table name	Origin	Description	Data content
State Databases Index	Drinking Water Database; WATUSE Database; and NPDES Database	Links the 3 State databases by providing for each user and their well, intake, or discharge pipe the permit number and unique record-identification number used in each State database	Name, permit numbers, STFID, town, county, latitude and longitude for each well, intake, and discharge pipe.
WaterUseGroupNHDemand	Seacoast Water-Use Database (Horn and others, 2008)	Water demand per employee by industrial SIC code; water demand by facility by type of commercial business	Description of business and estimated water demand.
SeacoastPerCapitaPerPWSID	Seacoast Water-Use Database (Horn and others, 2008)	Domestic per capita water demand by community water system as determined by the regression model in the seacoast area	PWSID and per capita value.
SystemWU	Drinking Water Database; WATUSE Database; NPDES Database; and other derived tables	2005 and 2020 estimated or reported demand by user	User permit numbers, name, description, population served, water-use code, facility or employee relationship, 2005 and 2020 demand estimate or reported value, STFID.
RegAllWuid	WATUSE Database	Reported withdrawal and return flow for registered users in 2005; estimated withdrawal and return flow for same users for 2020	User and source/discharge permit numbers, name, SIC code, facility or employee relationship, reported 2005 value and estimated 2020 value, latitude and longitude, STFID.
AssociationWater	State GIS data and Drinking Water Database	Relationship between STFID and CWS; used in determining population served in each census block	STFID, PWSID, WU_ID, 2000, 2005, and 2020 original population and 2000, 2005, and 2020 adjusted population served.
AssociationSewer	State GIS data and NPDES Database	Relationship between STFID and CWWS; used in determining population served by sewers in each census block	STFID, NPDES_ID, WU_ID, 2000, 2005, and 2020 original population and 2000, 2005, and 2020 adjusted population served.
Town Growth Rate	Census data (U.S. Census Bureau, 2001) and Population Estimates Database (NHOEP, 2007a and 2007b)	Town growth rates developed from the 2000 Census town population, the 2005 population estimates by town, and the 2020 population projections by town	Town name, growth rate from 2000 to 2005, and growth rate from 2000 to 2020.
TownSTFID	Census Database (U.S. Census Bureau, 2006) and GIS data sets	Relationship between STFID and town; used in applying town growth rate to census blocks	STFID and town name.

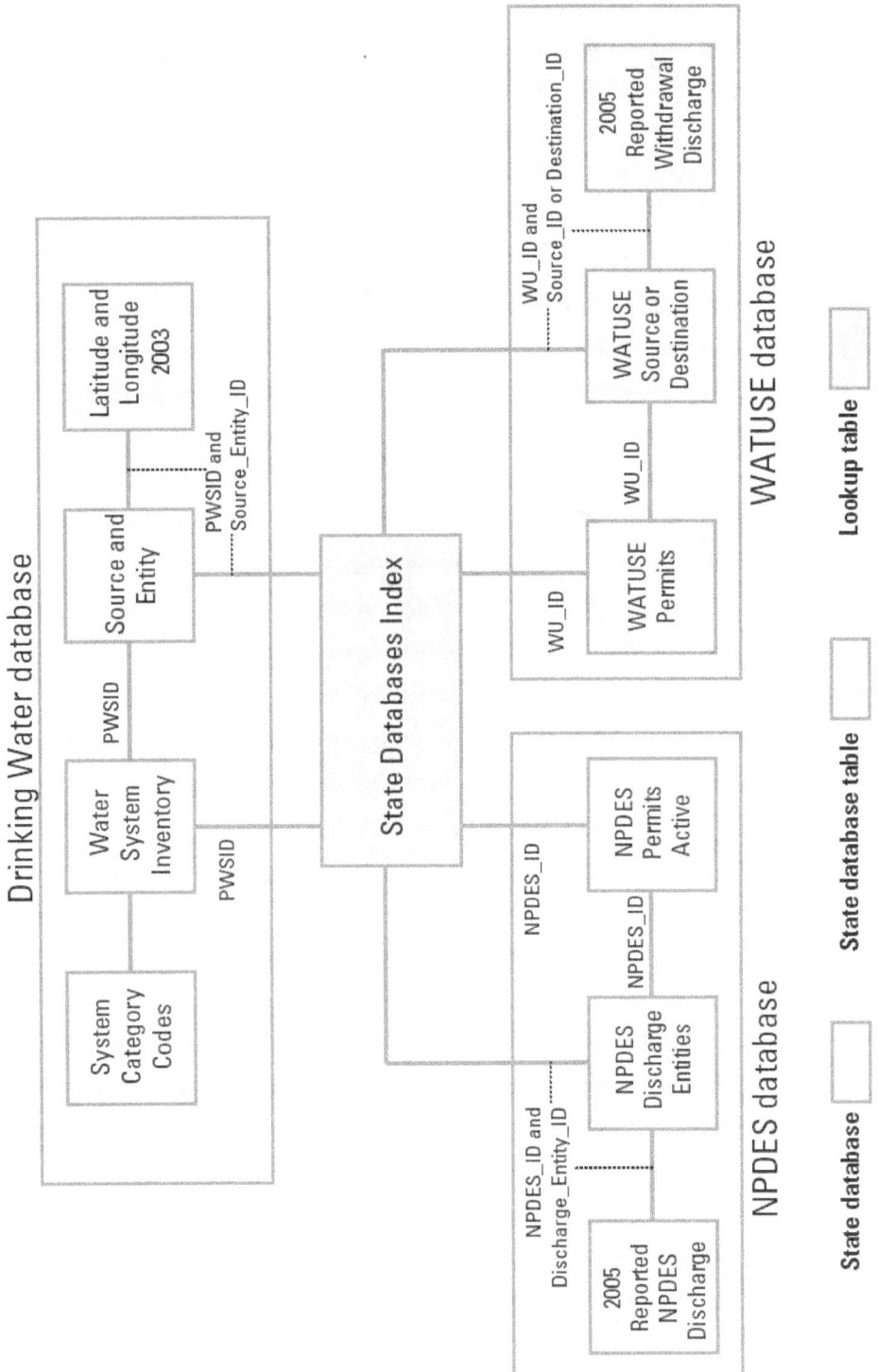

Figure 4. Table structure linking the Drinking Water, National Pollutant Discharge Elimination System, and Water Use databases in the New Hampshire Water Demand database.

[WATUSE, water-use database maintained by the New Hampshire Geological Survey; WU_ID, Unique number assigned to the water user in the WATUSE database; Source_ID, water source identification number in the WATUSE database; Destination_ID, wastewater destination identification number in the WATUSE database; PWSID, Public Water System identification number; Source_Entity_ID, water source identification number in the Drinking Water database; NPDES, National Pollutant Discharge Elimination System; NPDES_ID, National Pollutant Discharge Elimination System identification number; Discharge_Entity_ID, discharge point identification number in NPDES database]

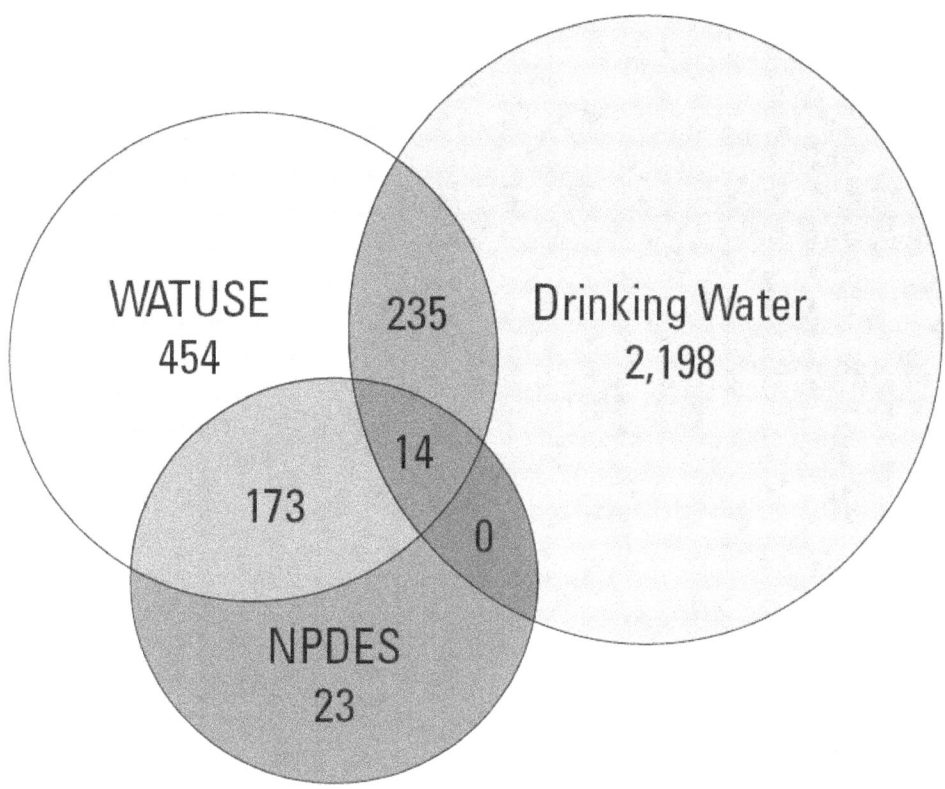

Figure 5   Results of matching the Water Use, Drinking Water, and National Pollutant Discharge Elimination System databases in the New Hampshire Water Demand database, in number of facilities.

database were identified using the latitudes and longitudes and descriptive names in the databases. This was complicated by the facts that the databases were not equally up-to-date and did not store the data in a parallel manner. The Drinking Water and NPDES databases contain unique withdrawal or return locations when more than one location exists for a facility. The WATUSE database provides only one discharge location per facility and, for some facilities, combines many wells and surface-water intakes into one source location. Therefore, the discharge points could not be matched and the number of sources matched was low. The total discharge amounts and locations from the WATUSE database were incorporated into the NH Water Demand database. When a one-to-one match was not made between sources in WATUSE and the Drinking Water database, the reported withdrawal obtained from WATUSE was apportioned manually among all sources listed as active in the Drinking Water database table.

Reported withdrawal and return flow values from the WATUSE database were used in estimating withdrawal and return flow for facilities not required to report to the state; the methods for estimating these flows are described in the

"Estimating Water Use by Census Block" section of this report. A small number of publicly supplied, non-domestic users that use less than 20,000 gal/d are not in WATUSE or the Drinking Water database. The return flow from this small number of users is not estimated. However, return flow from domestic users that are on public water supply but not on sewers is estimated using the methods described in the "Identifying Source of Water and Destination of Wastewater by Census Block" section.

Data from the Census database were integrated with the water-use data using the census block identification system. In the Census database, each census block is associated with a 15-digit unique identifier (STFID) composed of four geographic codes. For example, the STFID 330019501001000 is a concatenation of the State Federal Information Processing Standards (FIPS) code 33, the county FIPS code 001, the census tract code 950100, and the census block number 1000. The STFID is included in all tables that reference withdrawal and return-flow points for all nondomestic users, CWSs, and CWWSs in the NH Water Demand database.

Table 2.   Example from the State Database Index table showing fields used to link facilities and their source and (or) destination identification numbers among the Water Use, Drinking Water, and National Pollutant Discharge Elimination System databases.

[WATUSE, water-use database maintained by the New Hampshire Geological Survey; WU_ID, Unique number assigned to the water user in the WATUSE database; Source_ID, water source identification number in the WATUSE database; Destination_ID, wastewater destination identification number in the WATUSE database; PWSID, Public Water System identification number; Source_Entity_ID, water source identification number in the Drinking Water database; NPDES, National Pollutant Discharge Elimination System; NPDES_ID, National Pollutant Discharge Elimination System identification number; Discharge_Entity_ID, discharge point identification number in NPDES database]

Permit holder	Resource	Action	WATUSE database			Drinking Water database		NPDES database	
			WU_ID	Source_ID	Destination_ID	PWSID	Source_Entity_ID	NPDES_ID	Discharge_Entity_ID
Greenville Water Department	Reservoir 1	Withdrawal	20047	20047-S01		0991010	0991010-0000002	NHG640009	
Greenville Water Department	Reservoir 1	Return flow of filter backwash	20047		20047-D01	0991010		NHG640009	640009-001

Identifying the Source of Water and the Destination of Wastewater by Census Block

In order to estimate water withdrawal and return flow for each census block, the source of water and destination of wastewater for users in each census block had to be assigned. The latitude and longitude of each NCWS and CWS point of withdrawal were obtained from the Drinking Water database and associated with the appropriate census block. Similarly, the latitude and longitude of each CWWS point of return flow were obtained from the NPDES database and associated with the appropriate census block. To locate and quantify withdrawal and return flow for domestic users, the numbers of domestic users on self-supply, public supply, self-disposal (on-site disposal), and public disposal were estimated for each census block, so that the self-supply/self-disposal portions could be attributed to the census block in which the user resides. This was accomplished through the use of two GIS data sets: the NHDES Water Distribution and Sewer Collection Areas data set (Johnna McKenna, NHDES, written commun., 2003) and U.S. Census Bureau block data set (U.S. Census Bureau, 2006).

Water Distribution and Sewer Collection Areas GIS Data Set

NHDES created the polygon areas in the Water Distribution and Sewer Collection Areas data set by buffering the community water-distribution lines and sewer lines by 200 ft on each side. The data set was originally based on NH Department of Transportation (DOT) road locations, and the version used for this study was last revised in 2003. Areas of overlap between community water and wastewater systems are stored in the data set as single features with the attribute "pipe_type" set to "both." The PWSID for a CWS is associated with each contiguous water-distribution area that is part of the same system. The PWSIDs were used to link the Drinking Water database to this GIS data set. Links between this GIS data set and the NPDES database were established through the AssociationSewer table, described in the "Manual Adjustments to GIS Script Output" section of this report. Areas outside of the buffered lines were assumed to be self-supplied.

The Water Distribution and Sewer Collection Areas data set has limited accuracy for the following reasons:

- The water distribution and sewer collection lines have been buffered to depict areas and, therefore, capture some parts of other roads within 200 ft that are not served;

- The data set shows the entire system, including conveyances that extend from the source of supply to the distribution system and may cross roads that are not actually served by the system;

- Water distribution or sewer collection lines may have been extended since the last revision of the data set; and

- The buffered lines were based on the NH DOT road data set rather than the census road data set, which may result in some minor discrepancies with the census blocks.

Census GIS Data Set

The U.S. Census Bureau has been working to improve the accuracy of the digital line data that represent the roads, rivers, railroads, and other geographic features in their Topologically Integrated Geographic Encoding and Referencing (TIGER) database (U.S. Census Bureau, 2006). The Census Bureau relies on various Federal, state, local, and commercial data, including NH DOT data, to accomplish this goal. In December of 2006, the first available release of an updated digital line data set for New Hampshire was obtained, including the census block boundaries and the roads packaged by county (U.S. Census Bureau, 2006). The county data were converted from TIGER files to ArcGIS-compatible files and merged to create a statewide data set.

Together, the U.S. Census Bureau and the Water Distribution and Sewer Collection Areas data sets provided the means to estimate water withdrawal and return flow. The census population counts are associated with geographic areas (census blocks) that share geometry with the roads, and the water-distribution and wastewater-collection systems generally follow the roads. Therefore, overlays of the roads and water-distribution and wastewater-collection areas can be used to derive estimates of the number of domestic users per census block publicly supplied or self-supplied and the number that are on sewers or septic systems.

GIS Processing

In order to estimate domestic water withdrawal and return flow, estimates of the population served by CWS or CWWS in each census block were needed. The following assumptions were made to generate these estimates:

- Houses are not built along divided highways.

- Populations are evenly distributed along all other roads.

- The proportion of a census block's perimeter roads with water distribution lines is also the proportion of that census block's population served by water (and similar proportionality exists for sewer lines).

Therefore, calculating the length of each road segment that coincides with the water-distribution and wastewater-collection areas provides estimates of populations served by water and (or) sewer systems. From these lengths of road segments, proportions for each census block's perimeter (excepting highways) were calculated. Manual reviews of these calculations for quality-assurance purposes were conducted.

A preliminary GIS processing step identified all roads that form census-block boundaries and are associated with housing in order to use this subset of roads in subsequent GIS processing. All the TIGER linework is packaged in one file with each feature type (for example, road, railroad, physical feature, hydrography) noted in an attribute called "CFCC," or Census Feature Class Code (U.S. Census Bureau, 2007). Road features (CFCC starting with "A") were selected and saved to a separate file. Each line representing a road has a left and right side, defined by the direction of the line as it was originally drawn. As such, attributes stored in the road table include the state, county, tract, and 4-digit census block identification numbers of the polygons on each side of the road. In order to tie the road features to the 15-digit STFID in the tabular census data, the four attributes on the left side were concatenated to form a field called STFID_L, and four fields were concatenated to create STFID_R for the right side.

Any road segment with STFID_L not equal to STFID_R represents a road on the boundary between two census blocks. Road segments with CFCC starting with A1 are "Primary Highways with Limited Access." Roads on the outer perimeter of a census block that are not highways were selected and saved into a GIS data set of modified roads.

Road classes defined by the U.S. Census Bureau as one-lane dirt trails or roads typically inaccessible to motor vehicles also were examined in order to determine whether to exclude them from the analysis of population served. If few or no houses existed on these dirt roads, including them could invalidate the assumption that the population of each census block is evenly distributed on its roads. The analysis was run with and without these classes of dirt roads, and no difference in percent population served was observed.

A GIS script (program) was written that looped through each unique census block in New Hampshire and determined the proportion of people served by CWSs and CWWSs (fig. 6). During each iteration, first, the STFID, population, and housing-unit values of one census block were extracted and stored in variables for use in a subsequent analysis. Next, all census block boundary roads in the modified data set that surround that particular census block were selected (STFID_L or STFID_R equal to the STFID of the census block) and saved to a temporary file used for only one iteration. These roads were geometrically intersected with the Water Distribution and Sewer Collection Areas data set to add pipe type (water, sewer, both, or none), length, and PWSID attributes to the roads table. The lengths of all the roads in the temporary file were summed, and the lengths of each pipe type were summed.

A temporary table was created to store data gathered and calculated for each census block, including STFID ("STFID"), population ("pop00"), housing units ("hu00"), total length of roads ("rds_total"), length of roads with water only ("rds_water"), length of roads with sewer only ("rds_sewer"),

length of roads with water and sewer ("rds_both"), and the minimum and maximum PWSIDs ("minpwsid" and "maxpwsid"). To estimate the proportion of the population in that census block served by water, the proportion of length of water lines to total length of roads was calculated ("pct_water" = (rds_water + rds_both) / rds_total). Similarly, the length of sewer lines to the total length of roads also was calculated ("pct_sewer" = (rds_sewer + rds_both) / rds_total). During each iteration of the script, the row from this temporary table was added as a record to a comma-delimited text file resulting in a table with one row per census block (fig. 7).

If the roads in a census block were served by only one system or no systems, the minimum and maximum PWSIDs were the same. A record with minimum and maximum PWSIDs that differed indicated a census block that was served by more than one system; further analysis would be needed to determine how many systems serve that block and how to apportion the block's population among the systems.

A sample from the Water Distribution and Sewer Collection Areas data set and a table of calculated proportions for five example census blocks (highlighted with a yellow inner border) are shown on figure 7. Roads shown in black were included in the census block boundary data set; roads shown in gray were not. There is only one CWS in the town shown in figure 7, so "minpwsid" equals "maxpwsid" in all five example census blocks. In census block example number 2, the census block is bounded on the southwest side by a highway, which was eliminated from the analysis by the previously discussed assumptions. Consequently, the entire population of that census block was assumed to live along the other roads that compose the boundary, which is why the proportion served by water is close to 1.00 (or 100 percent) even though one side of the block has no CWS. Because of the inherent inaccuracies in the combination of multiple data sources, it was considered unreasonable to quantify the proportion of the population served by water or sewer more precisely than to the nearest 25 percent; the estimates were assigned to categories as shown in table 3.

Table 3. Percentages of census block population as assigned to 25-percent categories.

[CWS, community water system; CWWS, community wastewater system]

Percentage of census block's population with CWS (or CWWS)	Assigned category
0–10	0
11–36	0.25
37–63	0.50
64–89	0.75
90–100	1.00

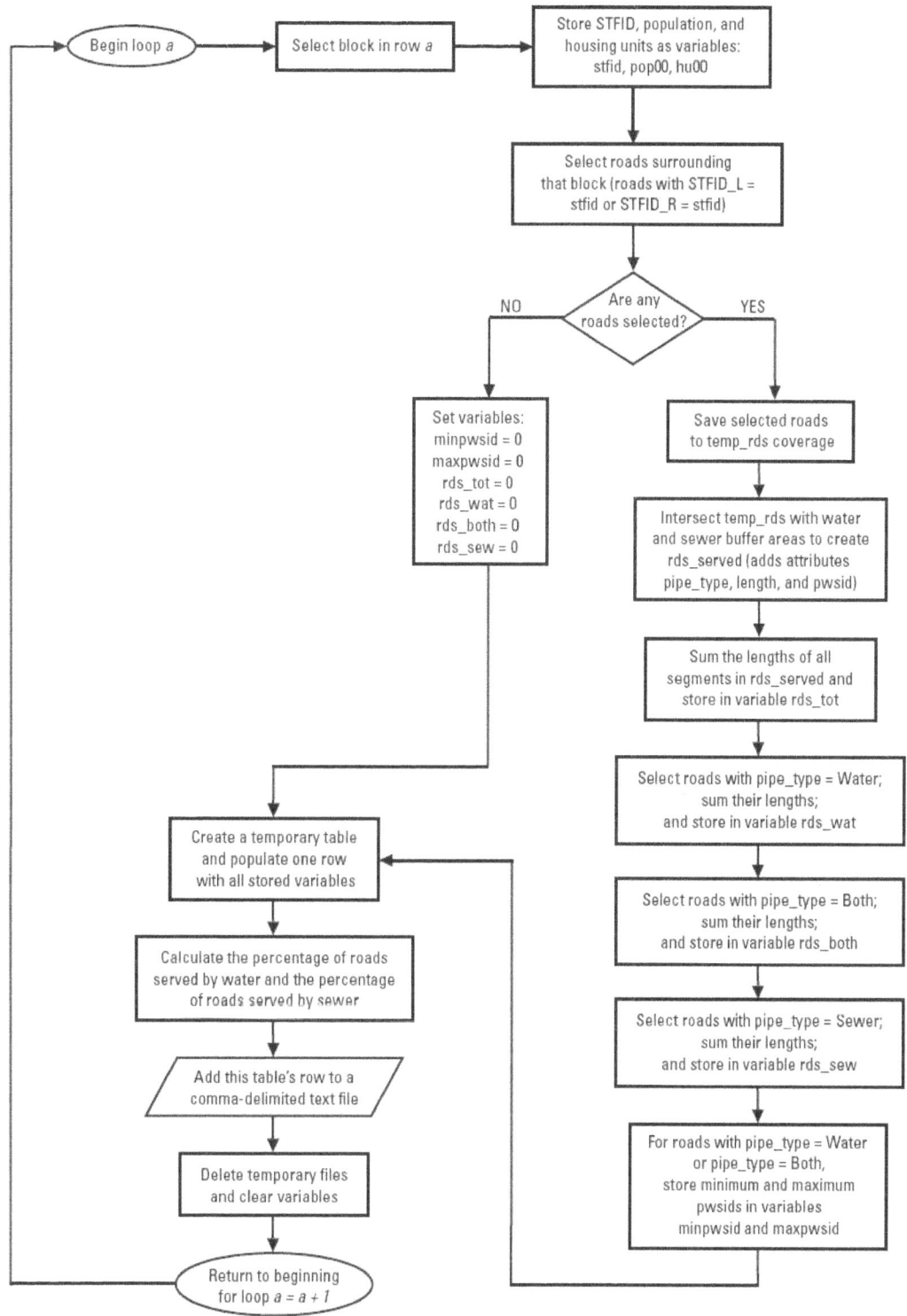

Figure 6.   Flowchart illustrating the logic followed to calculate the percentage of population in each census block served by water and (or) sewer.

[STFID, census block identification number; STFID_L, identification number of the census block on the left; STFID_R, identification number of the census block on the right; pop00, 2000 population count; hu00, 2000 housing unit count; pipe_type, attribute indicating whether that segment of road is served by water distribution, sewer collection, both, or neither; minpwsid, Minimum system identification number; maxpwsid, Maximum system identification number; rds_tot, Total length of roads; rds_wat, Length of roads inside "water" areas; rds_both, Length of roads inside "both" areas; rds_sewer, Length of roads inside "sewer" areas]

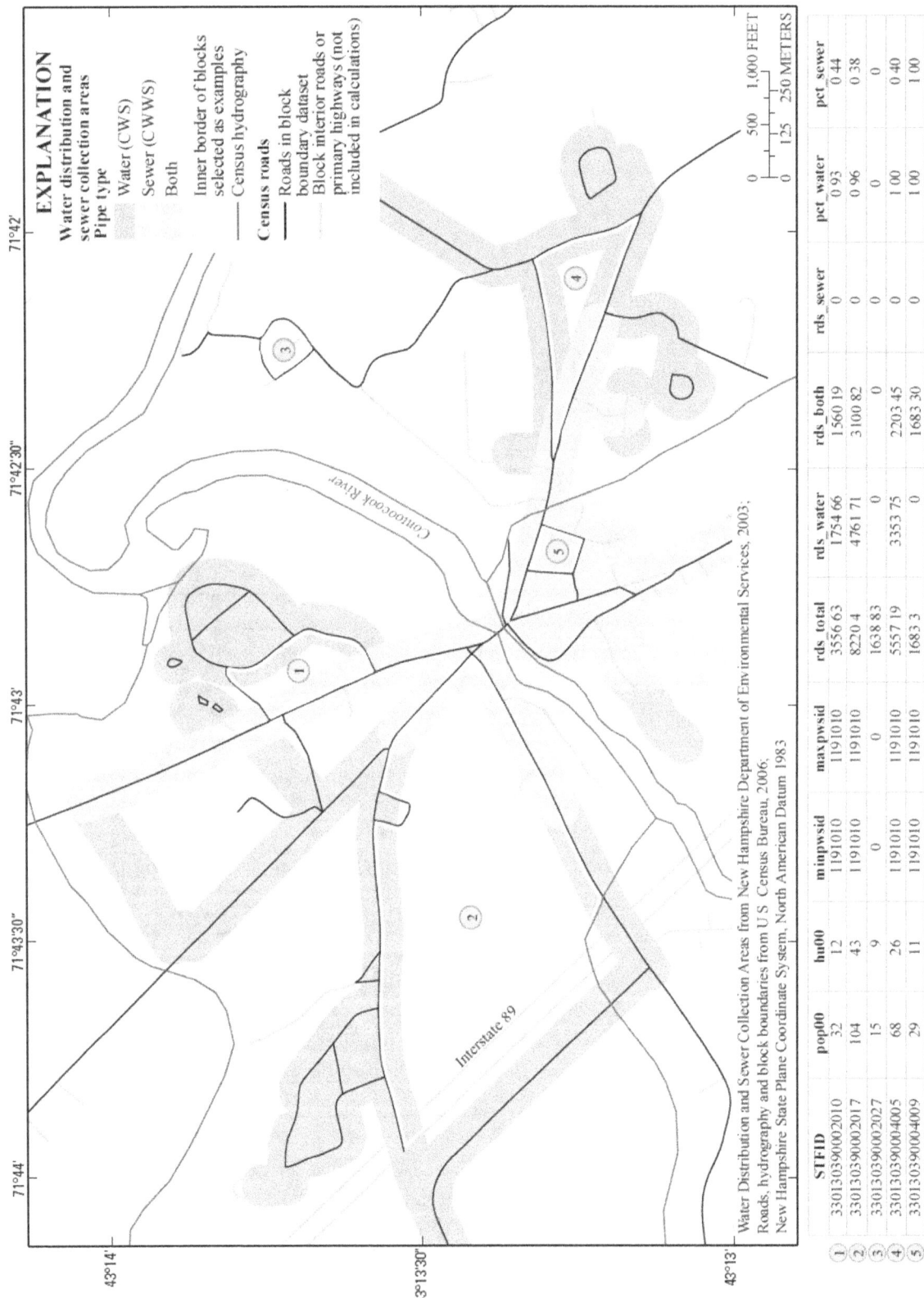

Figure 7. Examples of calculated proportion of the population in each census block served by water and (or) sewer to estimate withdrawal and return flow.

Growth Rate Calculations

For each MCD, the 2000 census population by town, population estimates from NHOEP for the year 2005, and population projections from NHOEP for the year 2020 were used to calculate growth rates from 2000 to 2005, from 2000 to 2020, and from 2005 to 2020 (New Hampshire Office of Energy and Planning, 2007a, 2007b). Reports by the NHOEP do not include unincorporated places, so the 25 unincorporated MCDs were assumed to have no increase or decrease in population and were assigned growth rates equal to 1.0.

In order to estimate domestic water demand, the estimated 2005 population in each census block was calculated as the 2000 census block population multiplied by the MCD growth rate between 2000 and 2005. Similarly, the projected 2020 population in each census block was calculated as the 2000 census block population multiplied by the MCD growth rate between 2000 and 2020. To estimate the 2020 water demand for registered users with reported 2005 values and unregistered, non-domestic users with 2005 estimates, the population growth rate from 2005 to 2020 was calculated and applied to those existing 2005 values.

Manual Adjustments to GIS Script Output

The table resulting from the automated GIS process contains records of estimated proportions of populations served by CWSs or CWWSs and the 2000 population. Additional records were needed to store the categories of estimated percentages for self-supplied users and users with on-site disposal, as well as the adjustments in population served when there is more than one CWS in the census block. Separate tables (AssociationWater and AssociationSewer) were created to analyze the source of supply and destination of wastewater. The steps in this process for the source of supply are shown in figure 8. (A similar process was used for the destination of wastewater). In the AssociationWater table, the fields minpwsid and maxpwsid correspond to the PWSID(s) serving the census block, and in the AssociationSewer table, these fields were changed to correspond to the NPDES_ID(s).

These "association" tables were manually revised to ensure that each census block had separate records to show self-supplied populations and each CWS that serves the census block. All the steps used to modify the output from the GIS script to the final version of the AssociationWater table are shown using the examples in table 4. An example row from the table resulting from the GIS script is shown at the top of table 4. Step 1 (shown in yellow in table 4 and figure 8) represents the initial creation of the AssociationWater table, which was accomplished by pulling some of the fields from the GIS output file.

Step 2 (shown in green in table 4 and figure 8) shows the fields Assoc_ID (unique record number), cat_pct (category percent with values of 0, 0.25, 0.50, 0.75, and 1.00), pop05

(estimated 2005 population), and pop2020 (projected 2020 population) that were added to the AssociationWater table. The Assoc_ID field is a unique record number automatically assigned as the record was added. The proportion of the population in that census block served by water, as calculated by the GIS script, was converted to a category percentage, according to table 3. Population estimates for 2005 and population projections for 2020 by census block were obtained from a table containing results of the growth rate calculations.

Step 3 (shown in blue in table 4 and figure 8) shows that a record was added for the self-supplied portion of a census block with at least one CWS, and another record was added if there was a second CWS. An initial value of zero in minpwsid indicated the entire census block was self-supplied, and the percent category was 1.00. When the value in minpwsid field was not zero, the value in cat_pct represented the portion of the population in that census block served by any CWS. A second record for that census block was added to the table to represent the self-supplied portion of the population, and its minpwsid was assigned 0. Because the publicly supplied and self-supplied portions must sum to 100 percent, the percent category in the new record was 1.00 minus the value in the first record. For example, if the percent category (cat_pct) was 0.25, then 0.75 was assigned to the self-supplied portion of the census block. In a census block with more than one CWS, the minpwsid was not equal to the maxpwsid in the AssociationWater table, so a third record was added to the AssociationWater table to represent the population served by the maxpwsid. The value in maxpwsid was assigned to the minpwsid field for that record. No population served value was associated with the second CWS at the time. Rarely, more than two CWSs serve the same census block. The approach used to identify other CWSs and to divide the population served among all the CWSs is described in the "Quality Assurance" section.

Step 4 (shown in orange in table 4 and figure 8) focused on calculating the population served by a CWS by multiplying the category percent by the 2000, 2005, and 2020 populations. First, however, the fieldname minpwsid was changed to PWSID and the field maxpwsid was removed from the AssociationWater table as it was no longer needed. (In the case of the AssociationSewer table, minpwsid was changed to NPDES_ID.) Then, the automatically adjusted self-supplied and CWS-supplied populations for 2000 were calculated by multiplying the percent category (0.00, 0.25, 0.50, 0.75, or 1.00) by the original 2000 population. The population values were rounded to the nearest whole number. The ratio of self-supplied users to publicly supplied users was assumed to remain the same for 2005 and 2020, so the same percent category was multiplied by the original 2005 and 2020 populations to create the automatically adjusted self-supplied and CWS-served populations for 2005 and 2020. Step 5 is described in the following section "Quality Assurance."

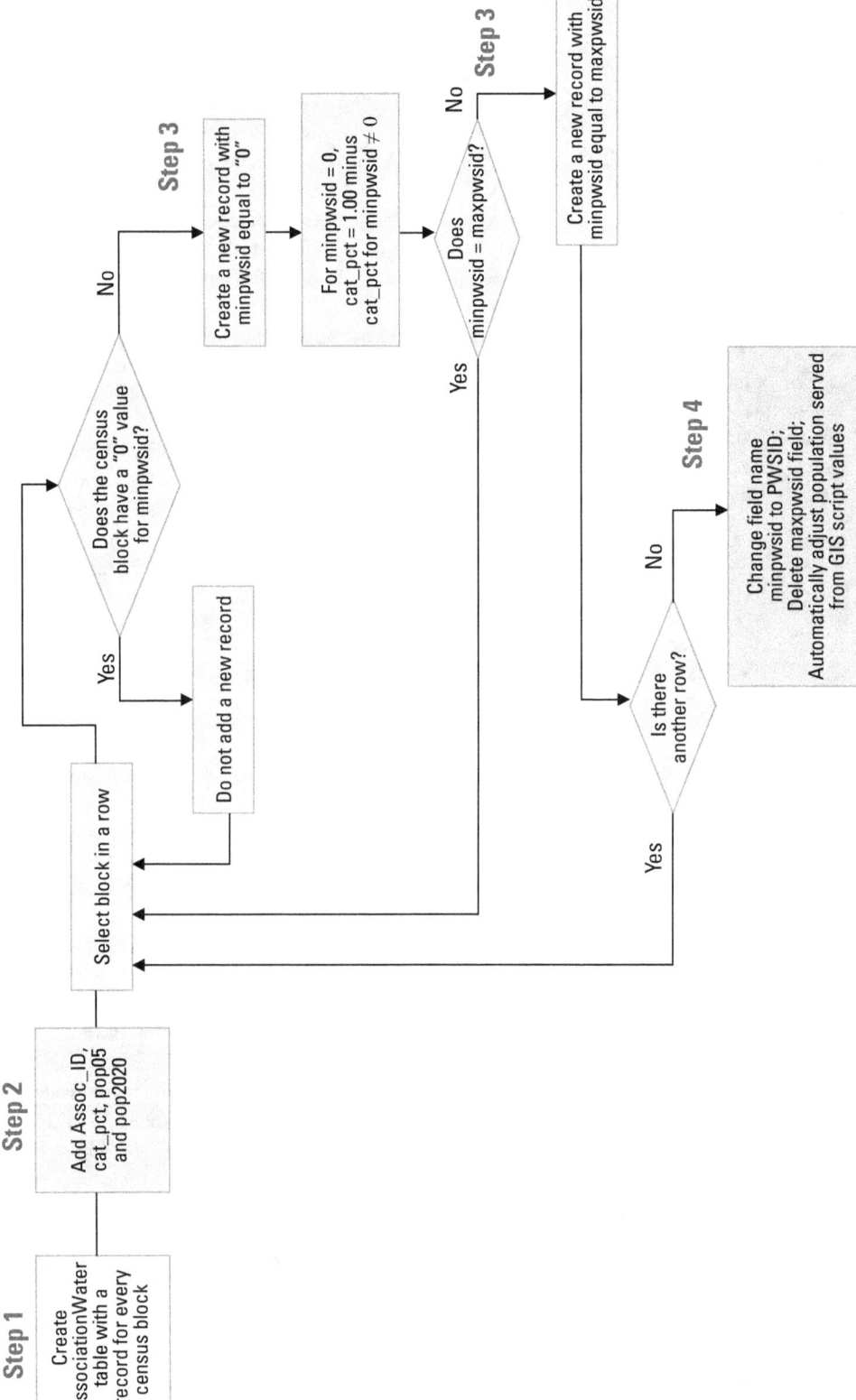

[GIS, geographic information system; Field definitions for table: Assoc_ID, unique record number for the AssociationWater table; cat_pct, category percent; pop05, estimated 2005 population; pop2020, projected 2020 population; minpwsid, minimum system identification number; maxpwsid, maximum system identification number; PWSID, Public Water System identification number; colored boxes relate the steps to those in table 4]

Figure 8.   Flowchart representing the process used to add records to the AssociationWater table to represent census blocks with multiple community water systems.

Table 4. Sample data from the AssociationWater table for a specific census block that is modified from the geographic information system script output to its final version by step.

[GIS, geographic information system; CWS, community water system; Auto, automatically; Colored entries indicate changes made during that step; Field definition for tables: STFID, Unique census block number; pop00, 2000 population count; hu00, 2000 housing unit count; minpwsid, Minimum system identification number; maxpwsid, Maximum system identification number; rds_tot, Total length of roads; rds_wat, Length of roads inside "water" areas; rds_both, Length of roads inside "both" areas; rds_sewer, Length of roads inside "sewer" areas; pct_water = (rds_water + rds_both)/rds_total; pct_sewer = (rds_sewer + rds_both)/rds_total; Assoc_ID, unique record number for the AssociationWater table; cat_pct, Percent category; pop05, 2005 population estimate; pop2020, 2020 population projection; PWSID, Public Water System identification number; Revised Category Percent Water, Whether the automatic value was adjusted; Status, Whether revision to this field was completed; Population 2000 Census Auto adjusted = 2000 population count calculated as percent category * 2000 population; Population 2005 Estimated Auto adjusted = 2005 estimated population count calculated as percent category * 2005 estimated population; Population 2020 Projected Auto adjusted = 2020 projected population count calculated as percent category * 2020 population; Population 2000 Census Manually adjusted, 2000 population count estimated for each census block; Population 2005 Estimated Manually adjusted, 2005 estimated population count estimated for each census block; Population 2020 Projected Manually adjusted, 2020 projected population count estimated for each census block]

Record as it comes from GIS processing script.

STFID	pop00	hu00	minpwsid	maxpwsid	rds_both	rds_wat	rds_tot	rds_sew	pct_water	pct_sewer
33015067001061	146	79	2232060	2232160	0	4640.11	8201.53	0	0.57	0

Step 1. Create AssociationWater table.

STFID	pop00	minpwsid	maxpwsid	pct_water
33015067001061	146	2232060	2232160	0.57

Step 2. Add fields.

Assoc_ID	STFID	pop00	minpwsid	maxpwsid	pct_water	cat_pct
28138	33015067001061	146	2232060	2232160	0.57	0.50

Step 3. Add records for self-supplied population and for maxpwsid.

Assoc_ID	STFID	pop00	minpwsid	maxpwsid	pct_water	cat_pct	pop05	pop2020
28138	33015067001061	146	2232060	2232160	0.057	0.50	164	184
47115	33015067001061	146	0		--	0.50	164	184
50810	33015067001061	146	2232160		--	--	164	184

Step 4. Calculate population served.

Assoc_ID	STFID	PWSID	Percent on any CWS	Category percent water	Revised category percent water	Status	Population 2000 Census Original	Population 2000 Census Auto adjusted	Population 2005 Estimated Original	Population 2005 Estimated Auto adjusted	Population 2020 Projected Original	Population 2020 Projected Auto adjusted
28138	33015067001061	2232060	0.57	0.50			146	73	164	82	184	92
47115	33015067001061	0	--	0.50			146	73	164	82	184	92
50810	33015067001061	2232160	--	--			146	--	164	--	184	--

Step 5. During quality assurance, adjust the population that is self-supplied or served by specific CWS.

Assoc_ID	STFID	PWSID	Percent on any CWS	Category percent water	Revised category percent water	Status	Population 2000 Census Original	Population 2000 Census Manually adjusted	Population 2005 Estimated Original	Population 2005 Estimated Manually adjusted	Population 2020 Projected Original	Population 2020 Projected Manually adjusted
28138	33015067001061	2232060	0.57	0.50	y	Done	146	89	164	100	184	105
47115	33015067001061	0	--	0.50	y	Done	146	20	164	24	184	35
50810	33015067001061	2232160	--	--	y	Done	146	37	164	40	184	44

Quality Assurance

Step 5 in table 4 (shown in purple) shows adjustments made during the quality-assurance process; the details of the process are shown in figure 9. A query was written linking the AssociationWater table with a list of active CWSs from the Drinking Water database to compare the population-served values from both sources. Review of the script-assigned percent categories was needed under any of the following conditions:

1. There were CWSs in the AssociationWater table that were not in the table of active CWSs from the Drinking Water database;

2. There were CWSs in the table of active CWSs from the Drinking Water database that were not in the AssociationWater table (for example, for census blocks with CWSs that only served populations on streets in the interior of the census block); and

3. The population served values in the AssociationWater table were less than 80 percent or more than 120 percent of the corresponding reported values in the Drinking Water database (which frequently occurred when there was more than one CWS serving populations in the census block).

The first test (fig. 9) was to determine whether there were CWSs in the AssociationWater table that were not in the table of active CWSs extracted from the Drinking Water database. When this occurred, Drinking Water Program staff were contacted to determine whether the inactive CWS was replaced by another CWS or not. If replaced, the PWSID of the current CWS supplying the census block was entered in the AssociationWater table in place of the inactive PWSID. If the inactive CWS was not replaced, the population became part of the self-supplied value.

The second test (fig. 9) was to determine whether there were active CWSs that were missing from the AssociationWater table. This could occur if a CWS was located on an interior road within the census block or if the CWS was established more recently than the GIS data set. The GIS script did not account for populations along streets interior to a census block (most commonly dead-end streets) that are supplied by different CWSs than those on the census block boundaries. This occurs primarily with small domestic-only CWSs. Inspection of the water-distribution areas in the GIS data set was used to identify the census blocks served by the CWS. In the instance where the CWS was established more recently than the GIS data set, the location of the CWS well(s) was used to identify the census blocks associated with the CWS. In both cases, new records were created for the CWS in each associated census block.

The third test (fig. 9) was to compare the estimated population served by each CWS to the reported value. This was done by dividing the automatically adjusted values (totaled for all census blocks served by the CWS) in the AssociationWater table (table 4, step 4) by the population served reported in the Drinking Water database. If the resulting ratio was less than 80 percent or more than 120 percent, all the census blocks associated with the CWS were evaluated. If any of these census blocks contained part of another CWS distribution system, all the census blocks associated with that second CWS were included in the evaluation. Ultimately, all CWSs and census blocks that were geographically interconnected with the originally selected CWS were identified and evaluated as a unit. An example of this situation using the census block included in table 4 is illustrated in figure 10. Table 5 provides one set of population-served estimates derived through this quality-assurance process.

The selected CWS from table 4, CWS 2232060, is associated with census blocks 330150670001061 and 330150670001060 (fig. 10). The automatically adjusted population served by this CWS in 2000 totals 76 (73 people in 330150670001061 and, not shown in table 4, 3 people in 330150670001060), which is 72 percent of the 105 population-served value obtained from the Drinking Water database. Because this ratio fails test 3 in figure 9, all associated CWSs and census blocks were examined (table 5). A second CWS, CWS 2232160, also serves people in 330150670001061. The GIS script calculated the proportion of the population served in the census block. So, for blocks with multiple CWSs, it was necessary to manually apportion the population served among all CWSs in the block. In order to do this, all CWSs that touch any of the census blocks associated with the selected CWS (2232060) were examined. This resulted in the list of all the CWSs and census blocks shown in table 5.

A perimeter road of census block 330150670001061 also coincides with the buffered area of CWS 2232150. It is not likely that any people within 330150670001061 are served by 2232150 though, because the overlap is merely an artifact of the buffering process. CWS 2232150 serves the interior roads of census block 330150670001067. The entire population served by that CWS (46) is attributed to 330150670001067, and the remainder of the population in that census block (109) is self-supplied.

CWS 2232160 touches four census blocks: 330150670001061, 330150670001062, 330150670001063, and 330150685002028. Neither 330150670001063 nor 330150685002028 contain any population, and 330150670001062 contains only population (85) served by CWS 2232160; therefore, the only census block requiring analysis is 330150670001061. The reported population from the Drinking Water database is 150, so the population in 330150670001061 served by CWS 2232160 would range from 37 (minimum to meet the goal of more than 80 percent) to 65 (maximum, if there are enough people available who are not accounted for by other CWSs).

CWS 2232060 touches three census blocks: 330150670001060, 330150670001061, and 330150685002027. Census block 330150685002027 does not contain any population served by CWS 2232060. The population in parts of 330150670001060 and 330150670001061

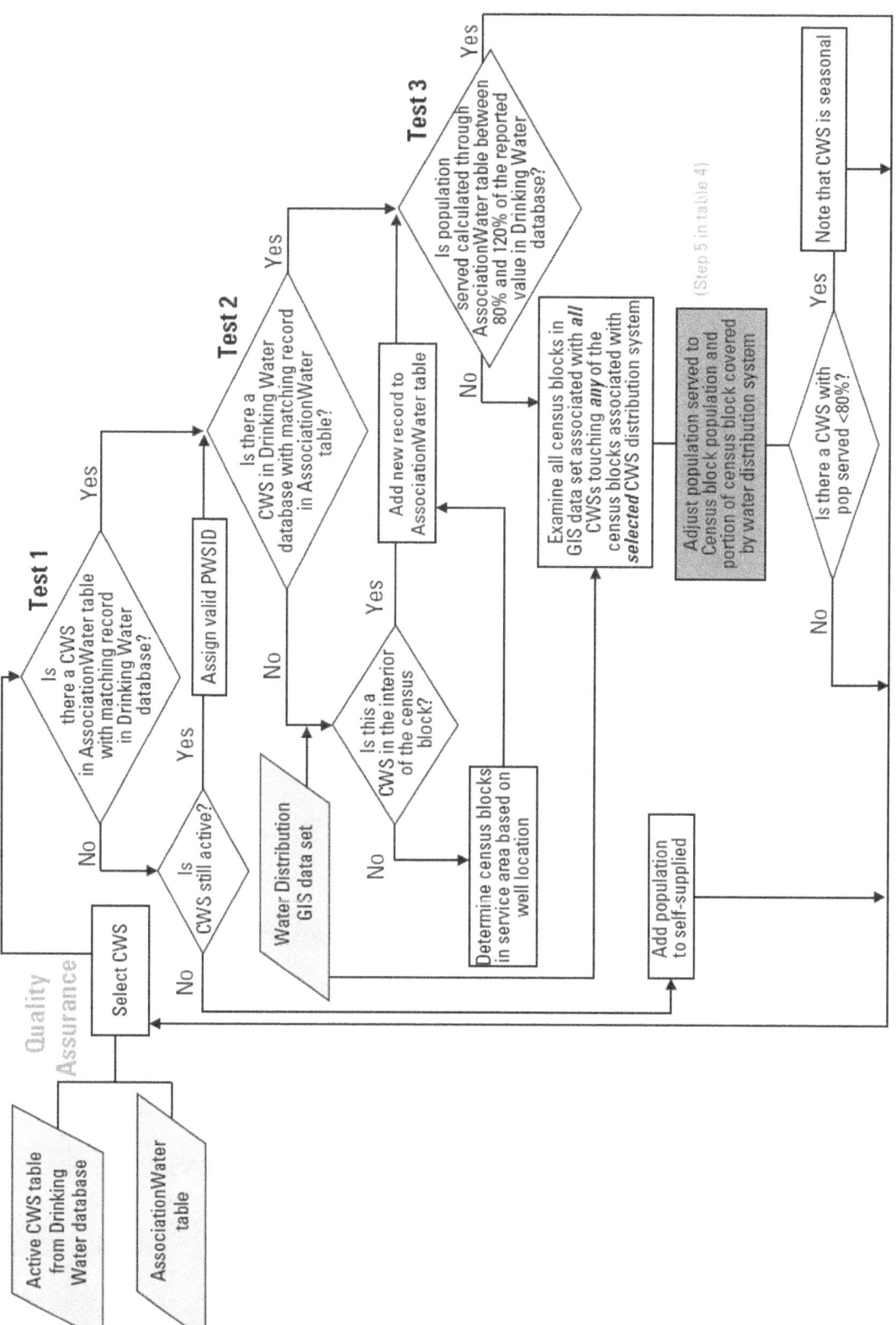

[CWS, community water system; GIS, geographic information system; PWSID, public water system identification number; <, less than; %, percent; pop, population; purple shade relates the step to that in table 4 and indicates the action step for this quality-assurance process]

Figure 9. Flowchart representing the quality-assurance process used to adjust population that is self-supplied or served by any community water systems in the census block.

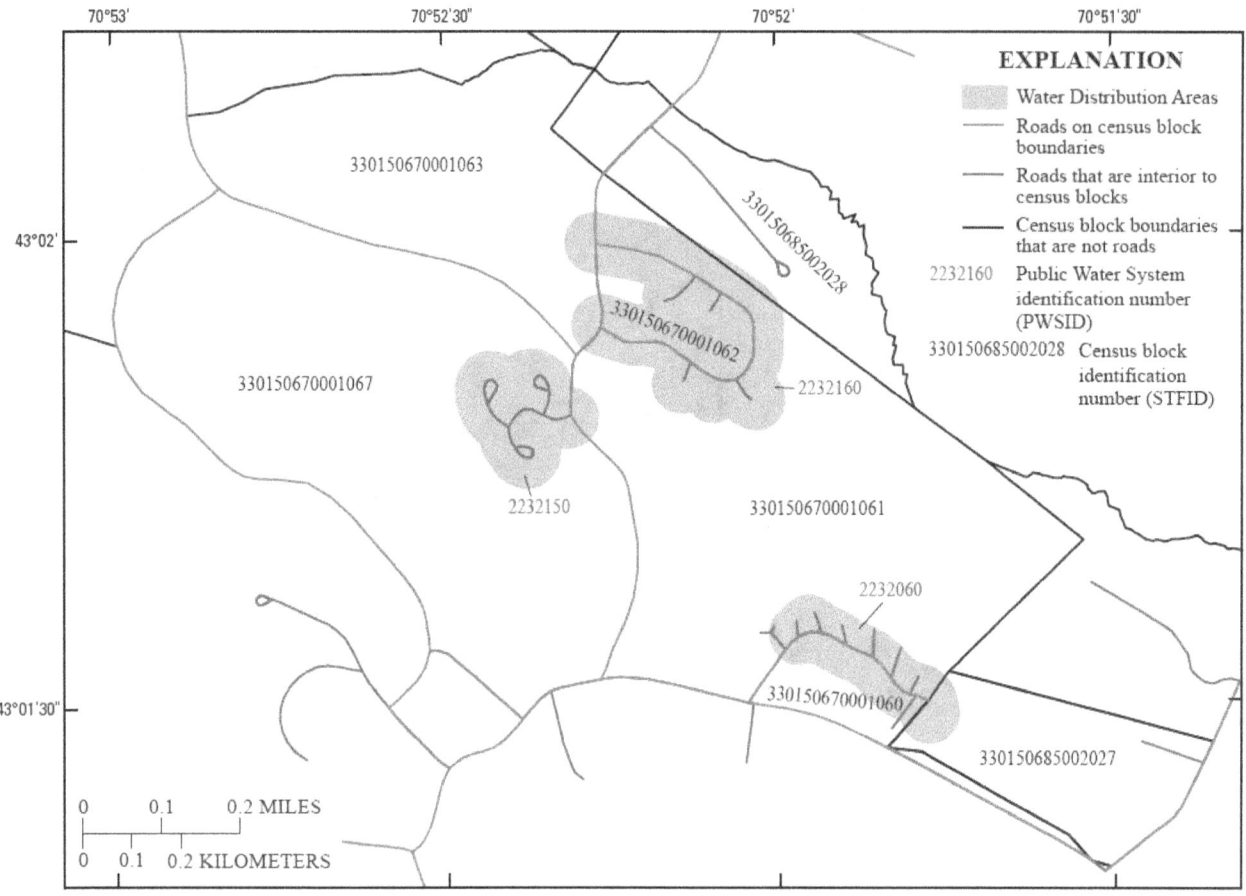

Water Distribution Areas from New Hampshire Department of Environmental Services, 2003
Roads and block boundaries from U S Census Bureau, 2006
New Hampshire State Plane Coordinate System, North American Datum 1983

Figure 10.   Example of a suite of community water systems and census blocks that are geographically interconnected.

then needs to number at least 85 (minimum to meet the goal of more than 80 percent) and at most 105 people (maximum, if there are enough people available who are not accounted for by other CWSs).

At this point, only two census blocks require adjustments: the population of census block 330150670001061 needs to be apportioned among CWS 2232160, CWS 2232060, and self-supply; and the population of 330150670001060 needs to be apportioned between CWS 2232060 and self-supply. Because census block 330150670001060 contains only six people and there is an interior road branching off the distribution area, all six are assumed to be served by CWS 2232060. CWS 2232060 needs at least 78 more people, CWS 2232160 needs at least 37 more people, self-supply needs some people, and the total cannot exceed 146. Balancing available population and road density in 330150670001061 yields a final break-down of 37 people for CWS 2232160, 89 people for CWS

2232060, and 20 people for self-supplied. Results are shown in table 5.

The procedure described above was used for most systems that failed test 3. Visual inspection of the spatial data was used to apportion the population in each census block among the different CWSs. On the basis of the road density in relation to the location of each CWS, the calculated population value was manually adjusted to reconcile the GIS-estimated population served with the reported population served. The previous assignments of census-block populations to CWSs in the New Hampshire Seacoast region (Horn and others, 2008) were incorporated into this study.

In some cases, test 3 could not be reconciled by the above process; that is, the estimated value could not be adjusted to one that was more than 80 percent of the reported value. In the majority of these cases, the CWS was seasonal and, therefore, the census population value used for the estimate did not reflect the summer-only population. The CWS was identified as seasonal.

Table 5. Quality-assured estimates of population served for a suite of interconnected community water systems and census blocks.

[CWS, community water system; Auto, automatically; yellow, orange, and purple shades refer to the steps in table 4; gray shade highlights the manually adjusted values]

Census block identifier	Total census block population	Population served						Total manually adjusted population	
		CWS 2232060		CWS 2232150		CWS 2232160			
		Auto adjusted	Manually adjusted	Auto adjusted	Manually adjusted	Auto adjusted	Manually adjusted	CWS-served	Self-supplied
330150670001060	6	3	6			0		6	0
330150670001061	146	73	89	0	0	0	37	126	20
330150670001062	85					85	85	85	0
330150670001063	65							0	65
330150670001067	155			0	46	16	0	46	109
330150685002027	56	0	0					0	56
330150685002028	43					0	0	0	43
Total from AssociationWater table	556	76	95	0	46	101	122	263	293
Total from Drinking Water database		105	105	46	46	150	150	301	
Ratio, in percent		72	90	0	100	67	81	87	

Estimation of Water Use by Census Block

The amounts of water demand, consumptive use, withdrawal, and return flow were estimated for 2005 and projected for 2020. Estimates of water demand and associated consumptive use were made using reported data from registered users and relations between water demand and ancillary data sets (Horn and others, 2008). These estimates of water demand served as the basis for estimates of groundwater and surface-water withdrawal. Estimates of return flow were calculated as water demand minus consumptive use. Projected population growth rates from 2000 to 2020 were applied in order to extend the water-use estimates to 2020 (New Hampshire Office of Energy and Planning, 2007b).

To estimate water demand where reported use or metered delivery data were not available, the relations between water demand and ancillary data were studied. In some cases (domestic and industrial use), this relation is expressed as a water-use coefficient. A water-use coefficient is an amount of water used per unit (for example, per person, household, or employee) and is multiplied by the number of units at the facility or within the area to obtain the total water demand for that facility or area. For example, if the domestic per capita water-demand coefficient is 75 gal/d and there are 1,000 people in the census block, the total domestic water demand is 75,000 gal/d in the census block. Coefficients are developed by analyzing the statistical relation between reported or metered water demand and ancillary data, such as population per housing unit, median value of homes, population density, number of employees at a specific facility, or units of product. To estimate commercial demand, a facility demand rate was developed through an analysis of the manner in which the water is used and the general size of the facility.

Assumptions

The following assumptions were made to estimate 2005 and 2020 water use:

- The 75 gal/d per capita and 16 percent consumptive-use coefficients derived during the Seacoast water-use study (Horn and others, 2008) can be applied to the entire State to estimate domestic withdrawal and return flow.

- The 2000 to 2005 and 2000 to 2020 town growth rates can be applied to each census block within the town to yield 2005 and 2020 population estimates for each census block appropriate for aggregating to larger geographic areas.

- The source of water and method of wastewater disposal do not change over time for any census block; that is, the same ratio of self-supplied to public supply is used for 2000, 2005, and 2020.

- Unregistered commercial and industrial self-supplied users that are outside the boundaries of CWWS collec-

tion systems as defined in the Water Distribution and Sewer Collection data set have on-site disposal; those that are inside the boundaries release wastewater into the collection system.

- The rate of water demand and consumptive use per person does not change over time; that is, coefficients developed for 2003 (Horn and others, 2008) are applicable for 2005 and 2020 estimates.

- Commercial water demand will increase at the same rate as domestic water demand in a census block; that is, commercial demand is tied to estimated population growth rates.

- Industrial water demand will not increase from 2005 to 2020 because increased industrial activity will be offset by more efficient use of water by new industries.

- Hydroelectric, thermoelectric, and irrigation demand for 2020 will be the same as 2005 reported values.

2005 Registered Use

Reported water withdrawal and return-flow data for 2005 for registered non-domestic users and most multi-use CWSs are stored in the WATUSE database. These data were integrated with the Drinking Water tables in the NH Water Demand database. The withdrawal values were linked to specific wells and surface-water intake pipes, and return-flow values were linked to discharge pipes. In some cases, it was necessary to estimate withdrawal values from specific wells or surface-water intakes because the reported withdrawal was for combined sources. These estimates were based on the total reported withdrawal divided evenly among all sources included in the reported total. Each source and discharge location was then associated with a census block in order to sum these water-use values and the estimates for unregistered users in each block.

2005 Unregistered Use

Domestic and non-domestic water withdrawal and return flow by unregistered users were estimated using two different approaches. Domestic water withdrawal estimates were based on the per capita water-demand coefficient applied to the portion of the population on self-supply. Estimates of domestic water return flow were calculated by subtracting the consumptive-use coefficient from the per capita demand coefficient and applying this coefficient to the portion of the population with on-site waste disposal. A different approach was required for estimating unregistered non-domestic water use due to the large variation in types of users. Non-domestic water withdrawal and return-flow estimates were based on water-demand and consumptive-use coefficients specific to the type of user.

Domestic Water Withdrawal and Return Flow

There are two types of domestic users: those that are self-supplied and those that are served by a small domestic-only CWS. The procedures for estimating the withdrawal by a domestic-only CWS are similar to those for self-supplied users, except for an additional step to link the total withdrawal for the system to the wells and surface-water intake pipes identified in the Drinking Water database.

Self-supplied domestic withdrawal in 2005 was estimated by multiplying the self-supplied population in each census block (estimated using the GIS script and quality-assurance adjustments) by the 75 gal/d domestic-demand coefficient from Horn and others (2008). Return flow for each census block was estimated using the estimated 2005 population with on-site waste disposal and the 63 gal/d domestic-return coefficient, derived by subtracting the 16 percent attributed to consumptive use from the demand (Horn and others, 2008).

An illustration of self-supplied withdrawal is shown as an example in figure 11. Each census block is classified according to the estimated self-supplied domestic withdrawal (in gal/day) divided by the size of the census block (in mi^2) to provide an indication of the intensity of the withdrawal in that area. A census block could have no self-supplied domestic withdrawals because there are no people living there, or because 100 percent of the census block population is publicly served.

Withdrawal by each small domestic CWS was estimated using the 75 gal/d water-demand coefficient and the estimated CWS 2005 population to compute a total demand for the CWS. The CWS demand was divided among all of its withdrawal points, and the withdrawal estimate was linked to the point(s). Each withdrawal location was associated with a census block by using its latitude and longitude coordinates. All return flow from the small CWS was assumed to be on-site waste disposal and included in the census-block total for return flow.

Non-Domestic Water Withdrawal and Return Flow

Non-domestic water withdrawal and return flow were estimated by assigning every non-domestic user to a water-use group that represents users with similar water-use characteristics. For any unregistered users, water demand can be estimated using a coefficient (for example, the food industry uses 469 gal/employee/day) or can be estimated per facility (for example, a small restaurant uses 1,000 gal/d). The water demand for each user was divided among and associated with the known withdrawal points. The return flow was estimated as 90 percent of the water demand and was collocated with the withdrawal site.

In order to characterize water demand, each of the 2,424 public water systems in the State was categorized into a water-use group related to Standard Industrial Classification (SIC) code. Determination of the appropriate water-use group for individual users was based initially on the user name. When the name of the facility alone did not allow for a water-use

group assignment, a search of the Internet often provided sufficient information to categorize the facility. For example, "Colley McCoy" and "1 Industrial Dr, Wyndam" yielded an Internet description that made it clear that this is a restaurant. There are 753 facilities (such as apartments, nursing homes, mobile home parks and others) categorized as community water systems (water-use group code 4941). Water demand was estimated using the 75 gal/d coefficient for any CWS that did not report its use. The 54 industrial facilities were grouped by 2-digit SIC code into 20 categories (table 6). The 1,617 commercial facilities were divided into 12 water-use groups (table 7).

Water-demand coefficients for the facilities in the industrial water-use groups in table 6 were developed by Planning and Management Consultants, Ltd. (1995) on the basis of water-meter readings at individual industrial facilities across the Nation (Horn and others, 2008). The range, median, and mean of these national coefficients and the number of facilities in NH in each category are shown in table 6.

Water demand for each of the 12 commercial water-use groups was estimated on the basis of facility size and types of activities (table 7). Commercial establishments with metered delivery data were grouped and subdivided by natural breaks in the magnitudes of meter readings. Specific water-related activities were identified that were likely responsible for the natural groupings, such as whether a school has a pool and whether a hotel has a restaurant. The unmetered commercial facilities were then grouped by general description (for example, hotels) and subgrouped by identifying the specific activities occurring at the facility (for example, hotels with restaurants). The median water demand values for the metered establishments in each subgroup were rounded and used for all commercial facilities in that subgroup (Horn and others, 2008).

2020 Projections

The amounts of water demand, consumptive use, withdrawal, and return flow by census block were estimated for 2020 in a manner similar to that used to estimate the 2005 values. Estimates of 2020 water use were based on the 2005 estimates or reported values and the projected population growth rates for 2020 for domestic and commercial demand. Industrial, hydroelectric, thermoelectric, and irrigation demand were assumed to remain constant. (See "Assumptions" section).

Withdrawal and return flow were estimated for 2020 by census block for self-supplied domestic users and domestic CWS users with the same methods used to estimate the 2005 values. The self-supplied and CWS-served populations within each census block were updated on the basis of the 2020 population projections, and withdrawal and return flow values were estimated on the basis of the 75 and 63 gal/d coefficients, respectively.

Non-domestic water withdrawal and return flow were estimated by increasing each commercial facility's 2005 demand by the town growth rate from 2005 to 2020.

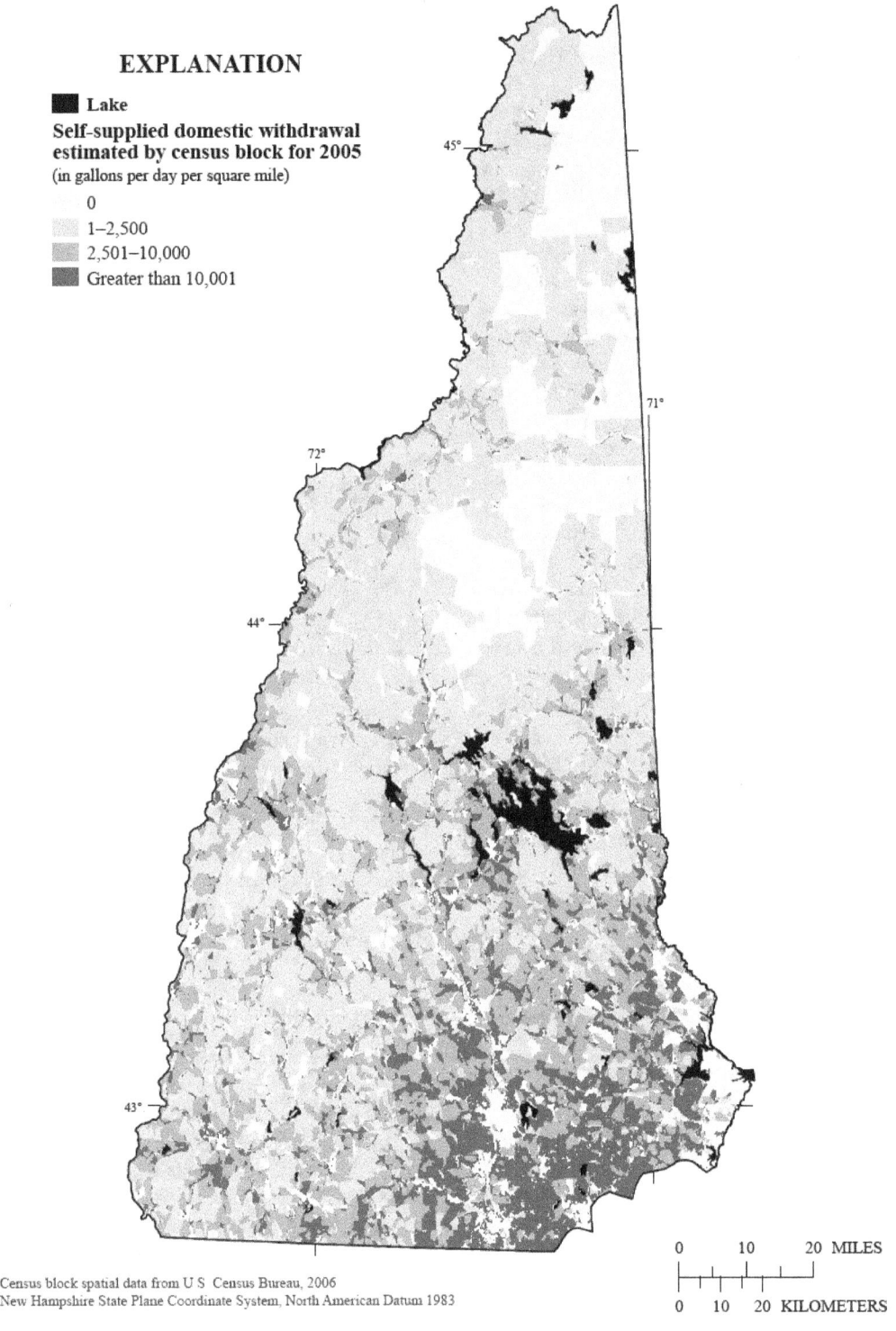

Figure 11.   The intensity of self-supplied domestic withdrawal estimated by census block for 2005 in New Hampshire.

Table 6. Coefficients for estimation of industrial water demand from two-digit Standard Industrial Classification categories and number of employees.

[Nonresidential employee water-demand coefficients are from Planning and Management Consultants, Ltd., 1995. --, no data available]

Two-digit Standard Industrial Classification category and [code]	Nonresidential employee water-demand coefficient (gallons per employee per day)			Number of facilities in New Hampshire
	Range	Median	Mean	
Industrial [20–39]	21–2,160	116	297	--
Food [20]	96–677	469	419	15
Tobacco [21]	--	--	217	0
Textile mill products [22]	246–1,076	315	521	1
Apparel [23]	6–43	13	21	0
Lumber and wood [24]	32–109	78	72	4
Furniture [25]	25–65	30	37	1
Paper [26]	114–8,304	863	2,160	3
Printing [27]	15–66	42	40	5
Chemicals [28]	128–653	289	363	3
Petroleum [29]	278–1,437	1,045	920	0
Rubber [30]	73–170	119	119	4
Leather [31]	--	--	148	0
Stone, clay, glass, and concrete [32]	13–224	202	147	1
Primary metal [33]	87–424	178	186	2
Fabricated metal [34]	48–585	95	189	2
Machinery [35]	28–153	58	70	7
Electrical equipment [36]	30–169	71	112	1
Transportation equipment [37]	14–143	63	78	1
Instruments [38]	40–141	66	72	3
Jewelry, precious metals [39]	27–61	36	39	1

Table 7.   Commercial facility water-demand estimates by water-use group.

[gal/day, gallons per day]

Water-use group code	Water-use group description	Population served range	Facility water-demand estimates (gal/day)	Number of facilities	Comments
5300	Retail stores	25–36	250	5	Population served reflects employees, not customers.
		43–70	500	4	
		40	750	1	
		125–173	1,000	3	
		200	1,500	1	
		400	2,500	1	
5411	Grocery stores	25–225	500	88	Facility water-demand value related to population served; population served for smaller numbers reflect employees rather than customers.
		250–999	1,000	25	
		30–395	2,000	7	
5812	Restaurants	25–250	500	106	Facility water-demand values are not based entirely on population served, as the population may mean those served during an hour, or over the course of a day. Other factors include whether the restaurant is seasonal or year round; sit down or take out.
		25–500	1,000	122	
		100–400	1,500	17	
		300–1,500	2,000	35	
		300–1,000	2,500	6	
7011	Motels and inns	25–138	500	113	Facility water-demand value related to population served, whether the facility has a restaurant, a pool, and (or) jacuzzis.
		30–50	1,000	3	
		48–300	1,500	26	
		115–5,000	2,500	5	
7032	Campgrounds and youth recreational camps	25–183	250	96	Facility water-demand value primarily related to water-using facilities available, the population served, and seasonal activity.
		15–657	500	212	
		55–650	1,000	78	
		665–1,350	1,500	4	
7600	Businesses	25–35	250	15	Facility water-demand value related to population served.
		35–60	500	36	
		60–75	750	10	
		75–600	1,500	26	
7800	Recreational facilities	20–2,500	250	64	Facility water-demand value primarily related to water-using facilities available, the population served, and seasonal activity.
		25–900	500	32	
		25–800	1,000	25	
		150–1,500	1,500	22	
		450–4,500	3,000	4	
7997	Golf courses	25	500	1	Facility water-demand value related to water-using facility available: snack bars, restaurants, showers, and irrigation systems.
		25–150	1,000	11	
		100–120	1,500	3	
		200	2,000	1	
		25–300	Reported	25	
8059	Health care facilities	40–50	500	3	Facility water-demand value related to population served.
		53–76	1,000	4	
		100–247	2,000	5	
8062	Medical offices and hospitals	25–70	500	10	Facility water-demand value related to population served.
		1,000	3,000	1	
8211	Schools and day cares	20–98	250	148	Facility water-demand value related to population served.
		60–85	500	3	
		99–325	1,000	82	
		335–730	2,000	56	
		750–2,500	6,000	19	
9000	Offices	15–49	500	32	Facility water-demand value related to population served.
		50–90	750	18	
		100	1,000	2	
		1,053	2,500	1	

Projected trends in commercial water demand were assumed to be strongly related to projected trends in domestic water demand—an increase in population leads to an increase in the commercial services needed for the population. Changes in CWS withdrawal and CWWS return flow from 2005 to 2020 were assumed to occur in proportion to the changes in projected population served as well. In the absence of data to indicate an increase or decrease in future demand, no change in industrial, irrigation, and other non-commercial demand was projected. It would be reasonable to assume that water demand associated with any increase in non-domestic, non-commercial activity likely will be offset by more efficient use of water by new facilities. The 2020 water demand for each non-domestic user was divided by the number of sources and associated with each withdrawal point. The return flow was estimated as 90 percent of the water demand and was collocated with the withdrawal site.

The increase in commercial demand probably will not occur as a growth-rate increase at each facility nor as a growth-rate increase within the census block. However, the growth-rate increase will likely occur at the town level or watershed level, depending on the size of the watershed. Therefore, the increase in commercial demand projected for each census block will not be as accurate as the commercial demand aggregated over a larger geographic area.

Summary

Methods were developed to estimate water use for 2005 and to project water use for 2020 throughout the State of New Hampshire by census block. The project was conducted by the U.S. Geological Survey, in cooperation with the New Hampshire Department of Environmental Services (NHDES), as part of a statewide study by NHDES relating water use to water availability. Estimates of water use rely on understanding what affects water demand and the associated consumptive use. The quantity of water needed for specific activities (demand) determines the quantity that is withdrawn, and the quantity of water that is returned to the hydrologic system after use depends on the quantity that is evaporated or otherwise removed from the system.

Water users in New Hampshire were identified using a combination of State and Federal data, which were integrated into the New Hampshire Water Demand database created for this study. The State databases yielded information on registered users, unregistered self-supplied non-domestic users, community water and wastewater systems (including population served and locations of points of supply and return flow), and population projections. Additional information on the size and type of unregistered self-supplied non-domestic users was obtained from the Internet. Domestic water users were enumerated and located using U.S. Census Bureau data for 2000, including census block population and housing-unit counts, census block boundaries, and roads.

Areas where withdrawal and return flow occur were determined by identifying the source of water and destination of wastewater for each user. The water source and disposal type were available in the State databases for non-domestic users but not for domestic users. Instead, water source and disposal type were determined for domestic users by comparing a data set from NHDES showing Water Distribution and Sewer Collection Areas to U.S. Census Bureau population and roads data. An algorithm was developed to automatically estimate the percentage of the population in each census block served by community water systems and the percentage served by sewers. The remaining portions were assumed to be self-supplied and have on-site disposal, respectively. All percentages were multiplied by the 2000 population, the estimated 2005 population, and the projected 2020 population in each census block. Manual adjustments of the estimates were made during the quality-assurance process. Summary tables of this withdrawal and return information are included in the New Hampshire Water Demand database.

The amounts of water demand and consumptive use for 2005 were estimated using data from the State database of registered users and results from a previous study in the Seacoast region of New Hampshire. The domestic-demand coefficient of 75 gallons per day from the Seacoast study was applied to individual users and unregistered domestic-only community water systems. Every non-domestic user was assigned to a water-use group representing users with similar water-use characteristics. Estimates of water demand for each commercial facility group developed during the Seacoast study were refined, and employee water-demand coefficients developed by Planning and Management Consultants, Ltd. were applied to each industrial facility by category. On the basis of these assessments, estimates of withdrawal and return flow were derived for the State. Projected population growth data from the State were used to develop a growth rate that was applied to domestic and commercial demand to extend the 2005 estimates to 2020.

References Cited

Horn, M.A., 2002, User's manual for the New England water-use data system (NEWUDS): U.S. Geological Survey Open-File Report 01–328, 377 p. (Available at http://pubs.water.usgs.gov/ofr01-328).

Horn, M.A., Moore, R.B., Hayes, Laura, and Flanagan, S.M., 2008, Methods for and estimates of 2003 and projected water use in the Seacoast Region, southeastern New Hampshire: U.S. Geological Survey Scientific Investigations Report 2007–5157, 87 p., plus 2 appendixes on CD-ROM (Available at http://pubs.usgs.gov/sir/2007/5157).

New Hampshire Department of Environmental Services, 2006, Scope of the NPDES Program: NHDES Environmental Fact Sheet WD–WEB–21, 5 p. (Available at http://des.nh.gov/organization/commissioner/pip/factsheets/wwt/documents/web-21.pdf).

New Hampshire Geological Survey, 2007, Water use registration and reporting in New Hampshire: New Hampshire Department of Environmental Services Environmental Fact Sheet CO–GEO–4, 2 p. (Available at http://des.nh.gov/organization/commissioner/pip/factsheets/geo/documents/geo-4.pdf).

New Hampshire Office of Energy and Planning, 2007a, 2005 Population estimates of New Hampshire cities and towns, accessed January 11, 2007, at http://www.nh.gov/oep/programs/DataCenter/Population/PopulationEstimates.htm.

New Hampshire Office of Energy and Planning, 2007b, 2010–2030 Population projections for New Hampshire municipalities, accessed January 11, 2007, at http://www.nh.gov/oep/programs/DataCenter/Population/PopulationProjections.htm.

Planning and Management Consultants, Ltd., 1995, IWR-MAIN Water demand analysis software, User's manual and system description, version 6.1: Carbondale, Ill., 497 p.

U.S. Census Bureau, 2001, Census block demographics Summary File 1 (SF1) for New Hampshire, accessed September 17, 2003, at http://arcdata.esri.com/data/tiger2000/tiger_download.cfm.

U.S. Census Bureau, 2006, 2006 Second Edition TIGER/Line Files, accessed December 15, 2006, at http://www.census.gov/geo/www/tiger/tiger2006se/tgr2006se.html.

U.S. Census Bureau, 2007, 2006 Second Edition TIGER/Line Files Technical Documentation: Washington, D.C., 353 p. (Available at http://www.census.gov/geo/www/tiger/tiger2006se/TGR06SE.pdf).

U.S. Environmental Protection Agency, 1998, SDWA Section 1401(4) Public Water System Definition as Amended by 1996 SDWA Amendments: Federal Register, v. 63, no. 150, Notice, p. 41939–41946, accessed January 5, 2006, at http://www.epa.gov/safewater/pws/pwsfrn.html.

Glossary

A

Aggregate of users   A group of users defined by a geographic area, such as state, county, minor civil division, or Hydrologic Unit boundary, for which withdrawal, distribution, use, consumptive use, wastewater collection, or return flow are collectively estimated.

C

Census block   The smallest geographic area for which the U.S. Census Bureau collects and tabulates data. A census tract is subdivided into census block groups, which are subdivided into blocks.

Coefficient   *See* water-use coefficient.

Commercial water use   Water used for motels, restaurants, office buildings, ski resorts, water parks, and other commercial facilities and institutions. The water may be supplied by a community water system or be self-supplied.

Community wastewater system (CWWS)   Wastewater collected from users or groups of users, conveyed to a wastewater-treatment plant and released as return flow into the hydrologic environment or sent back to users as reclaimed wastewater.

Community water system (CWS)   System for the provision to the public of water for human consumption through pipes or other constructed conveyances if such a system has 15 year-round service connections or serves more than 25 year-round residents. Community water systems provide water for a variety of uses, such as domestic, commercial, industrial, thermoelectric power, and public use.

Consumptive use   That part of withdrawn water that is evaporated, transpired, incorporated into products or crops, consumed by humans or livestock, or otherwise removed from the immediate water environment.

Conveyance   The systematic and intentional flow or transfer of water from one point to another primarily during distribution and wastewater collection.

D

Delivery   The amount of water delivered to users.

Discharge pipe   A pipe through which effluent is released after use into a receiving stream or infiltration bed. Also referred to as an outfall.

Distribution   The process of conveying water from the community water-system points of withdrawal or treatment through the distribution system to the user or another water supplier. Water is "released" from the community water system into the distribution systems and "delivered" to users. *See also* Delivery and Release.

Distribution system   A pipe or system of pipes conveying water from wells and intake pipes or a potable water-treatment plant to users. A local distribution system conveys water to users within a single minor civil division. A regional distribution system conveys water to users in more than one minor civil division or to another regional distribution system.

Domestic self-supplied withdrawal estimate   For this statewide study, the population within a census block that is self-supplied was multiplied by the average annual per capita water demand (75 gallons per day) derived from the Seacoast water-use study.

Domestic septic return flow estimate   For this statewide study, the population within a census block that uses a septic system was multiplied by the average annual per capita water demand (75 gallons per day, derived from the Seacoast water-use study); then the amount of consumptive use (16 percent, derived from the Seacoast water-use study) was subtracted.

Domestic water use   Water for household purposes, such as drinking, food preparation, bathing, washing clothes and dishes, flushing toilets, and watering lawns and gardens. Households include single and multi-family dwellings. Also called residential water use. The water may be obtained from a community water system or be self-supplied.

E

Export   Water that is removed from an area (watershed or town) for use in another area, or wastewater that is removed after use from an area (watershed or town) for treatment and release in another area.

G

Geographic information system (GIS)
A computer system capable of capturing, storing, integrating, analyzing, and displaying geographically referenced information.

Groundwater return flow   Wastewater that is returned to groundwater over a geographic area by an aggregate of users or through septic systems.

Groundwater withdrawal   Water that is withdrawn from groundwater over a geographic area by an aggregate of users or by a single user for which there is not enough information to select a more specific site type.

I

Import   Water that enters or is brought into an area (watershed or town) for use, or wastewater that is conveyed after use from an outside area (watershed or town) for treatment and release in the area of interest.

Industrial water use   Water used for industrial purposes, such as fabrication, processing, washing, in-plant conveyance, and cooling, and includes such industries as steel, chemicals, paper, and petroleum refining. The water may be supplied by a community water system or be self-supplied.

Intake pipe   A pipe in a surface-water body through which water is diverted to another site.

Interbasin transfer   Conveyance of water across a drainage or river-basin divide.

Irrigation water use   The artificial application of water to lands to assist in the growth of crops or pasture including greenhouses. Irrigation water use also may include application of water to maintain vegetative growth in recreational lands, such as parks and golf courses, including water used for frost and freeze protection of crops.

L

Leakage   Water that moves from a conveyance system or storage area into the surrounding and underlying materials. This process will occur if the ambient groundwater pressure is less than the internal pressure of the conveyance system or storage area at a breach.

M

Mining water use   Water used for the extraction of naturally occurring minerals including coal, ores, petroleum, and natural gas. Includes water associated with quarrying, milling, and other onsite activities done as part of mining. Excludes water used for processing, such as smelting and refining, or slurry pipeline (industrial water use). These activities are included in Standard Industrial Classification (SIC) codes 10–14.

Minor Civil Division   A political or administrative area of a county or county equivalent, other than an incorporated place, established by appropriate state or local government authorities and adopted as a primary county division; equivalent to a town in New England.

N

Non-community Water System (NCWS)
A water system that serves people either temporarily in residence (transient), as at a motel or restaurant, or regularly using the drinking-water supply without actually living at the site (nontransient), as at a business.

P

Per capita water use   The average volume of water used per person during a standard time period, generally per day.

Potable treatment plant   A site that prepares water to drinking-water standards through processes including chlorination, fluoridation, and filtration.

Projected water demand   Estimates of future water demand generated using estimates of future population or employee number and current (2003) water-demand coefficients.

Public use   Water supplied from a community water system and used for firefighting, street washing, water-treatment plant backflushing of filters, and municipal parks and swimming pools.

R

Registered user   In New Hampshire, a user who withdraws, receives, or uses water or releases or returns wastewater at a rate of 20,000 gallons per day or more over any 7-day period.

Release   Water discharged by a user or group of users into a wastewater-collection system.

Resource   Aquifer or surface-water body from which water is withdrawn/diverted or returned.

Return flow   Water that is returned to surface-water or groundwater resources after use or wastewater treatment and, thus, becomes available for reuse. Return flow can go directly to surface water, directly to groundwater through an injection well or infiltration bed, or indirectly to groundwater through septic systems.

S

Self-supplied water   Water withdrawn from a groundwater or surface-water source by a user and not obtained from a community water system.

Sewage disposal (septic) system   Refers to a buried tank for the separation of solids, grease, and liquid components of wastewater in the absence of oxygen. The liquid fraction from the septic tank is discharged to a drain field and the solids remain in the tank for later disposal as septage.

Single user   An individual user for which withdrawal, use, consumptive use, or return flow are measured or estimated. This place of use can be a manufacturing plant, commercial facility, or irrigation field.

Standard Industrial Classification (SIC) code   Four-digit codes established by the U.S. Office of Management and Budget and used in the classification of establishments by type of activity in which they are engaged.

Surface-water return flow   Wastewater that is returned directly to an unknown surface-water body or wetland, or occurs over an area such as from irrigation or meltwater after snowmaking. This does not include water discharged into ponds for holding or percolation purposes.

Surface-water withdrawal   Water that is withdrawn from surface water over a geographic area by an aggregate of users or by a single user for which there is not enough information to select a more specific site type.

T

Transfer   *See* water transfer or interbasin transfer.

U

Unaccounted-for water   Water supplied from a community water system that has not been accounted for as being distributed to domestic, commercial, industrial, or thermoelectric uses. It includes public water use (fire fighting, street washing, water-treatment plant backflushing of filters, and municipal parks and swimming pools), leakage (conveyance loss), and meter errors.

Unregistered CWS withdrawal estimate   For this statewide study, the population served by the CWS was multiplied by the average annual per capita water demand (75 gallons per day) derived from the Seacoast water-use study.

Unregistered user   In New Hampshire, a user who withdraws, receives, or uses water or releases or returns wastewater at a rate of less than 20,000 gallons per day over any 7-day period.

W

Wastewater   Water that carries wastes from homes, businesses, and industries; a mixture of water and dissolved or suspended solids.

Wastewater collection   The process of conveying wastewater from users through a wastewater-collection system (sewer system) to a wastewater-treatment facility. May also include storm runoff. Wastewater is released by the user into the collection system and received by the treatment facility. Wastewater also can be released from a local collection system into a regional collection system.

Wastewater-collection system   A pipe or system of pipes conveying wastewater from users to a wastewater-treatment plant. A local collection system conveys wastewater from users within a single minor civil division. A regional collection system conveys wastewater from users in more than one minor civil division or from another regional collection system.

Wastewater-treatment plant   Plant that prepares wastewater for discharge into the hydrologic system through the removal or reduction of contained solids or other undesirable constituents.

Water demand   (1) Water required to meet specific water-use needs, such as for domestic, commercial, or industrial purposes. The term is used in this report in connection with projections of current use into the future. (2) Relation between water use and price, when all other factors are held constant; that is, increased prices result in decreased water use. (3) Demand is a general concept used by economists to denote the willingness of consumers or users to purchase goods, services, or inputs to production processes, because the willingness varies with the price of the thing being purchased. (4) Refers to the schedule of water quantities that consumers would use per unit of time at a particular price per unit.

Water supply   All the processes that are involved in obtaining water for the user before use, including withdrawals, water treatment, and distribution.

Water transfer   Artificial conveyance of water from one area to another.

Water use   Water use pertains to human interaction with and influence on the hydrologic cycle and includes activities such as water withdrawal, distribution, consumptive use, treatment, wastewater collection, and return flow.

Water-use coefficient   An amount of water used per unit (for example, per person, household, or employee) for each category of use.

Withdrawal   The removal of surface water or groundwater from the natural hydrologic system for use, including community water systems, industry, commercial, domestic, irrigation, livestock, thermoelectric power generation, mining, and other off-channel water uses.

Prepared by the Pembroke Publishing Service Center.

For more information concerning this report, contact:

Director
U.S. Geological Survey
New Hampshire-Vermont Water Science Center
331 Commerce Way, Suite 2
Pembroke, NH 03275
dc_nh@usgs.gov

or visit our Web site at:
http://nh.water.usgs.gov

USGS